T4-ADO-541

NOW IS YOUR TIME TO WIN

by Dave Dean
with Marti Hefley

Tyndale House
Publishers, Inc.
Wheaton, Illinois

"One Day at a Time"
by Marijohn Wilkin and Kris Kristofferson.
© 1973 Buckhorn Music Publishers, Inc.,
P.O. Box 120547, Nashville, TN 37212.
International copyright secured. All rights reserved.
Used by permission.

First printing, March 1983

Library of Congress Catalog Card Number 82-51199
ISBN 0-8423-4724-0
Copyright © 1983 by Dave Dean
All rights reserved
Printed in the United States of America

To Suzie
A gift from
God

CONTENTS

Foreword by Og Mandino 11
Principle 1: Accept Your Situation 13
Principle 2: Be Willing to Fail 29
Principle 3: Make Daily Preparations 45
Principle 4: Be a Professional 61
Principle 5: Live in the Present 81
Principle 6: Do Your Best 99
Principle 7: Let God Help You 117
To the Reader 128

ACKNOWLEDGMENTS

With deepest gratitude I acknowledge those who have played such an integral part in *Now Is Your Time to Win:*

The Southwestern Company for sixteen great years of association and for providing such an excellent testing ground for the seven principles shared in my book.

Bob Wolgemuth for putting me in touch with Jim Hefley.

Jim Hefley for encouraging me to pursue my book project.

Susie Littleton, Paul Martin, and Dan Moore for their very helpful suggestions.

The many people who so willingly granted the interviews used throughout the book.

Mary Kay Ash, Jerry Heffel, Charles "Tremendous" Jones, David J. Schwartz, Ph. D., W. Clement Stone, and Zig Ziglar for reviewing my book.

Og Mandino for his foreword and the inspiration I have received from his friendship and writings.

Vicki T. deVries for her expert editing and willingness to go the extra mile.

Wendell Hawley and Tyndale House for publishing *Now Is Your Time to Win.*

Joyce Crosslin, my secretary, for her many years of dedicated service.

Mom and Dad for their guidance and encouragement which have made such a lasting impact on my life. Special appreciation to Mom for her valuable input on my book.

My wife, Suzie, for her abiding love and support and for her invaluable help in typing the manuscript.

Marti Hefley, a truly professional writer, for her patience, persistence, and expertise which have made *Now Is Your Time to Win* a reality.

Foreword

Reading this book will be a waste of your time.

Reading this book will be a waste of your time unless you are determined to change your life for the better, beginning right now. Not tomorrow or next week or next month. Now!

This marvelous volume, in one way, is its own worst enemy. Most books on selling, old and new alike, are dull. Reading them usually drains the most ambitious salesperson's positive mental attitude as he or she struggles through the usually obligatory chapters dealing with every step of the salesperson's routine from prospecting to closing. To get anything worthwhile out of most books on selling, one has to work very hard at staying awake.

Now Is Your Time to Win presents you with a different kind of challenge. Not only is its brilliant author, Dave Dean, one of the nation's leading sales trainers, but he also happens to be a compelling writer! That's the problem and you should be forewarned.

From the book's opening sentence, you will be swept up by the trials and travails of this gutsy man's efforts to master the art of selling. And since he tells his story in such an honest and easy-to-read style, the danger is that you will miss the thrust of his seven principles and lose yourself in this book as good entertainment.

So, how can you get the most from this gold mine you hold in your hand?

Read it through, the first time, for pure enjoyment. As you do, you will gradually begin to realize that you are in the presence of a very special professional who has been through every selling rejection and tribulation you have, and then some, and who has, through trial and experience, devised seven basic principles of selling and living that will change you from "average" to "leader" once you begin following them.

Percy Whiting, Dale Carnegie's managing director for so many years, once wrote, "Any fool can learn from experience. It takes a smart salesman to learn from a book—and it pays." *Now Is Your Time to Win* will pay off for you in many ways.

It will certainly increase your commissions. It will put your career in proper perspective. It will launch you toward a career in sales management, if that is your goal. Most important, it will make you proud to be a salesman or a saleswoman, one of the most difficult, and yet most rewarding, professions on this earth.

This book will change many lives. What it does with yours is up to you.

Og Mandino

PRINCIPLE 1

Accept Your Situation

I knew who he was and why he had come. Numbly I handed over the car keys to the bank representative and watched him back my full-equipped Buick Riviera out of the driveway and drive into the autumn sun. The car blended with the fall colors as it disappeared into the distance. That car had been the last symbol of my success, and now even it was gone.

I couldn't believe this was happening to me. I had been riding so high—the kid with the golden touch. At age nineteen I had made $7,500 selling books one summer. In 1967 that had seemed like the pot at the end of a rainbow, the good-luck talisman that insured a life of continued success. Now, just two years later, I not only had been stripped of my most prized possession, but also was $14,000 in debt.

Dazed by the reversal in my circumstances, I staggered back into my apartment as if I were in a dream. My situation seemed so unbelievably hopeless and I felt so depressed that I began to understand how a person could turn to drink or drugs or even commit suicide.

Now Is Your Time to Win

The idea of paying back what seemed at the time to be such an overwhelming amount was devastating. I had no job, no tuition money for my last semester. I wasn't doing well in school, my self-image was punctured, and my confidence was shot. Someway I had to graduate so I could get a decent job, but even if I managed that, it would take me years just to get even financially.

Bankruptcy went through my mind, but I just couldn't take that route since I'd talked close friends into cosigning my notes. As the days progressed, I retreated from my problem by sleeping more and more, hoping I'd wake up and find it was all a bad dream.

If I had been told at that point that I could bounce back from failure to success in *thirty seconds,* I wouldn't have believed it, and I would probably have thought my intelligence was being insulted.

The summer between my junior and senior years in college, I had invested all my savings and $14,000 in borrowed money in a cosmetics company. I had been led to believe I could clear $50,000 the first year. Instead, the pyramid-type operation of the company had been declared illegal, and I was left holding an empty moneybag. I'd already sold my Corvette to pay my fall tuition. Yet I returned to Taylor University in Upland, Indiana, and continued to play the part of the successful entrepreneur even though I was broke except for pocket money and a few dollars in a checking account.

Even after my second car had been repossessed, I kept trying to carry off the role, but with a student body of only 1,200, that was no easy task. When friends would ask about my difficulties, I'd just grin

Principle 1: Accept Your Situation

and say, "Oh, I've just had a little setback. Nothing serious." I might have fooled some of them, but my creditors knew better.

Christmas vacation came, but I couldn't afford the plane fare to California to be with the family. Instead, I went to Kentucky, stayed with a friend, and sold soap door to door, earning only fifty dollars for the week's work. That sure wasn't going to pay the tuition for my last semester, and I was facing the necessity of dropping out of school.

My place of refuge during those dark days was the nearest Pizza King. Manager Ben Hodgin and his wife, Carolyn, demonstrated an inordinate amount of patience by letting me hang around night after night for hours at a time. The atmosphere was warm and friendly, but most importantly Ben and Carolyn would sit and listen to my tale of woe without judging my stupidity or berating my fate. "OK, turkey, so you blew it," Ben would agree, "but look, you can pull out of this if you just keep your cool." Instead of sympathy, he gave me a job delivering pizzas and mopping floors.

Taylor's Coach Bob Davenport, former two-time All-American from UCLA, took time to counsel me. It really helped to be able to talk frankly about my situation. Except for my roommates, I was still trying to give my fellow students and professors the impression that I was still on top. With Bob I could be open about my situation.

"You can overcome this," Bob assured me. "And someday you'll look back at this as one of your greatest learning experiences."

I had great respect for Bob and his strong belief that I could bounce back helped to bolster my self-image and to redirect my thinking. A short time later a phone call came from Glenn Jackson, my former sales manager at The Southwestern Company.

"I've heard you've got a little situation," Glenn said.

"Yeah, I really have."

"Is there anything I can do to help?"

"Not unless you have $14,000 to $15,000 you don't need." I laughed.

"I heard you're considering dropping out of college."

"I don't want to, but I don't have a choice. I don't have money to repay my debt and can't borrow more. I wouldn't want to borrow more if I could."

"How much would you need to get you through your final semester?"

"A thousand would probably do it."

"OK, Dave, you'll have a check for that amount in the mail Monday morning."

"Glenn, I don't know how or when I'll be able to pay you back."

"Don't worry about that, Dave. Pay me when you can. Now, this is what I want you to do. First of all, quit feeling sorry for yourself. You'll pull out of this, but you need to finish college first. Right now you need to go to your creditors and assure them that you intend to pay back everything you owe, even if it is just a small amount weekly or monthly. Explain your situation to them. David, you've got to quit ignoring the problem."

"Should I sell books again this summer?"

"I don't know. That's your decision. But you and I both know it would probably be your best bet for that three-month period of time."

Principle 1: Accept Your Situation

"Glenn, I don't know how to thank you."

"Don't try."

I hung up the phone and sat there reviewing the conversation in my mind. Glenn was sending me $1,000 with no strings attached. What a vote of confidence! He had also given me some excellent advice. Now was the time to accept my situation exactly the way it was. Nursing my wounded ego, whining about my humiliation, and wallowing in self-pity all these months had not helped. All the principles I had learned about being successful weren't working for me because I was not accepting my situation the way it was. I was trying to put my life back together without first laying the proper foundation. Before I could make any progress, I had to quit daydreaming that my debt would somehow miraculously disappear and start facing my problem honestly.

Honestly. That word gripped me. Honestly facing my problem would mean I would no longer have to try to pretend I was a success. It didn't mean that I had to be satisfied with the mess. And I sure didn't like it, but if I had guts enough to accept it and make the commitment to do whatever was necessary to pull out of it, I could go on from there. I could quit trying to fool my friends. I could call my folks and tell them about my financial fiasco. I breathed a deep sigh. Honestly accepting my situation brought me a sense of relief. It seemed that a burden had been lifted from me, and I could feel my old enthusiasm coming back.

As objectively as I could, I considered my liabilities and my assets. There was really only one big liability: "The Debt." On the positive side I had a family that loved me. Excellent health. I had friends like Ben and Carolyn and Bob and Glenn, who still believed in me.

If I really cracked the books, I'd soon have a college degree. With 3,000 hours of sales experience gained by knocking on 8,000 doors, I'd had a lot more experience than most of my contemporaries. I'd had a taste of success, and even though the climb out of debt looked rough and would take a long time, I was excited because I had just taken the first step.

As I look back on that experience now, I realize just how big a step accepting my situation really was. I've also learned in the intervening twelve years that I'm not the only one who has had to take that step. After a friend and I had finished playing a couple of sets of tennis with my brother, Doug, and a country music personality he travels with quite often, I asked the singer how he had turned his career around.

Just a few years previously, after he'd been seventeen years in his profession, his group had dissolved and he was broke, thousands of dollars in debt, and perplexed about his future. He accepted his situation, determined to return to doing those things that had worked when his career was doing better.

"I went back to the basics," he told me. That must have been the right decision. Kenny Rogers is doing better now.

I had the privilege of interviewing Colonel Harlan Sanders for my radio talk show, "The Winners' Circle," just a few weeks before he died at age ninety-one. He was an excellent example of a man who refused to be defeated by circumstances. When he was sixty-two years old, a new highway had wiped out his restaurant business. He could have gone to Florida

Principle 1: Accept Your Situation

and spent the rest of his life in a beach chair, bewailing his bad luck. He didn't. He accepted his situation exactly the way it was. The traffic was gone. The business was dead. He took inventory of what he had left and decided he had a pretty good recipe for fixing chicken.

"I had a friend who had a restaurant in Salt Lake City," Colonel Sanders reminisced for me. "In twelve years in business he'd never sold fried chicken, and I couldn't interest him in trying mine. It took some doing, but I finally convinced him to eat some. He kinda smiled when he took his first bite and nodded at his wife. He started selling chicken like it was going out of style. Couldn't keep up with his booming business.

"That was my first franchise. After that, one franchiser would tell another what my chicken had done for him. In two years I had 600 franchises. There are now over 6,000 in fifty-four countries.

"That highway moving away from my place was one of the best things that ever happened to me," Colonel Sanders mused. Here was a man who hadn't spent much time worrying about circumstances he couldn't control. He had accepted the situation and turned the negative circumstances into one of the greatest business successes of our time.

It's only natural to feel down when circumstances seem to be going against you. But even in the most difficult of times, if you're willing to accept your situation exactly the way it is, you can bounce back. One of the young men who attended the sales school held each summer at The Southwestern Company was faced with seemingly insurmountable odds. Two weeks before he had come to Nashville, his fiancée had dropped him cold, and a week later his mother had died. He came on to sales school anyway. When he picked up his check at the end of the summer, he ranked as one of the top out of the 3,500 first-year salespeople.

"Dave," he told me, "I can honestly say that half the mornings before I started knocking on doors, I was in tears. I never felt more alone in all my life, but I had made a commitment, and I felt I should keep it. And I did."

He could have spent the summer feeling sorry for himself, and everyone would have understood, but instead he bravely accepted his situation, kept his commitment, and won over the odds.

Mary Kay Ash is well known because of the tremendous success of Mary Kay Cosmetics. Shortly after plans had been made to start the business, her husband died of a heart attack. She had depended on him for the administration and financial ends of the business. Mary Kay could have dropped the plans for a new direct-selling business in cosmetics, and no one would have blamed her. She didn't. She accepted the situation and went on to build one of the fastest-growing companies in the country.

Mary Kay suffered another tragic loss. Mel Ash, her second husband of fifteen years, died of lung cancer a few weeks before I interviewed her. Shortly after I entered her luxurious home in Dallas, Mary Kay was reminiscing about Mel. "He was a wonderful man who went everyplace I went," she said. "He called himself the 'father of 70,000 daughters.' When he died, I was scheduled to be in a jamboree with my salespeople four days later. I went because I had

Principle 1: Accept Your Situation

committed myself to being there, and I knew that was where Mel would have wanted me to be."

Mary Kay Ash has not allowed hardship, tragedy, and numerous difficult circumstances to defeat her. In each instance she has accepted her situation and has become stronger as a result.

In 1968 my good friend Jerry Pogue was a district sales manager with The Southwestern Company when he had a tragic boating accident that almost took his life. He was hospitalized for two-and-a-half months, and lost the use of one arm until seven operations over many years. Instead of allowing the accident to ruin his career, he returned to work just as soon as he could.

Jerry went from recruiting 150 salespeople the year before the accident to 200 the next year. The following year, in 1971, he recruited 417 salespeople. The year after that, he built an organization of 665 people and set a recruiting record that still stands. He went on to become senior vice-president of The Southwestern Company, earning well over six figures annually. In the nine years we worked together, I never once heard Jerry complain about his misfortune.

Jerry is now in the investment business in Seattle as a stockbroker. While talking to Jerry recently, I wasn't surprised to hear that between February 1980 and July 1981, he had opened over one thousand new accounts totaling approximately $7 million in the worst bear market that the precious metals market had ever seen. Jerry Pogue has learned to accept his situation no matter what it is and has continued to commit himself to being a winner.

Now Is Your Time to Win

Over lunch one day John Wooden, famed basketball coach and winner of ten national titles, talked with me about his early years.

"When I came to UCLA, basketball was not well thought of. Strict academic entrance standards prevented us from acquiring some of the best players. I was led to believe that UCLA's Pauley Pavilion would be completed within three years, and instead it took seventeen. I conducted practice during those years on the third floor of an old gym with the wrestlers and gymnasts practicing on the sidelines, and at the other end of the floor people were working out on the trampolines. Besides these distractions, for seventeen years my managers and I had to sweep and mop the floor every day before practice because the dust would make it dangerous for the players.

"These conditions were rather difficult, and I let them bother me for quite a while. As a matter of fact, I was at the point of developing a persecution complex. Eventually, when I accepted them, I came to realize you have to do your best with the things you can control and not spin your wheels on things you cannot control. I changed my attitude, and we went on to win the first two of our national championships under those same conditions."

Jeanne Robertson is an excellent example of a young lady who took stock of a circumstance she could not change and turned it into an asset. "In the seventh grade, at thirteen years of age I was 6'2" tall," she told me. "Now, all thirteen-year-old girls seem to have problems, but this wasn't one that was going to go away. My parents were great about it, though, and helped me have a positive outlook. They helped me anticipate remarks that people were sure to make.

Principle 1: Accept Your Situation

Then we'd come up with a comic response. This really helped me to develop a sense of humor about my height, and I still use many of the lines we developed in my speeches. I might as well face the fact that even though I might live to be 103, I'll never be a 'little old lady.'

"One advantage I had was that I grew up in a basketball area in North Carolina. I started playing in the fifth grade and played all through high school and college. The things you cannot change, you have to accept."

The tallest lady ever to have competed in the Miss America pageant and winner of the Miss Congeniality award, she is now in great demand as a professional speaker. She is earning top money in a demanding field because she learned to accept her situation, and has used it to her advantage. She is frequently billed as "a tall gal with a tall sense of humor."

At the National Speakers Association Convention where I first met Jeanne, I also met John and Greg Rice, twin brothers who are very successful businessmen from Florida. While having dinner with them, I asked for one of their business cards. The name of their company is THINK BIG. "The name expresses our philosophy of life," John explained to me. "We hold motivational seminars and challenge people to 'think big.' "

Naturally I asked them how they'd gotten started doing these seminars. "First, we decided to go into the real-estate business," Greg recalled, "so we took a one-week crash course, got our licenses, and started selling in West Palm Beach, Florida. Together we sold fifty-eight houses that first year, setting a record for the company we were working for. Before long we were being asked to speak to groups of realtors, and the seminars resulted."

John had given a speech in Garden Grove, California. A representative of NBC-TV's "Real People" had been in the audience and had asked them to do the show. "This led to more TV appearances and roles in the TV series 'Foul Play,'" John explained. "We've just signed a contract to do a new game show which all three major networks are bidding for."

The Rice brothers continue to be willing to accept themselves as they are. This, in spite of the fact that soon after they were born their parents abandoned them. John and Greg Rice "think big" and are great men even though each stands just 2′ 11-1/2″ tall.

I was discussing the recent depressing times in the real-estate market with my friend Janet Ballas, one of the top real-estate salespersons in the metropolitan Washington, D.C. area and a twenty-year veteran in the field. She told me, "OK, so the real-estate business is tough right now, but it just shows you what you are made of. They say, 'When the going gets tough, the tough get going,' and that's really true. I'm having some of my best months ever, but I'm having to work longer hours to do it. You've got to accept the challenge. I'm going to reach the top, regardless of circumstances. If it weren't high interest rates, it would be something else.

"It's a matter of taking a negative and counteracting it with a positive. If I worry about the client I just lost, I will lose the next two, so I don't worry about it. I try to learn from past mistakes, but I never live in the past. There's just nothing you can do about it. I erase negative thoughts."

Principle 1: Accept Your Situation

With an attitude like that, it's no wonder Janet continues to produce year after year, and is a lifetime member of the Million Dollar Club. This exclusive membership is limited to those who have sold at least a million dollars' worth of real estate annually for five consecutive years.

I have a good friend by the name of Mort Utley who, at age fifty-nine, lost his complete net worth in the real-estate recession of 1974: $3 million. "I learned a lot through that experience!" he declared enthusiastically. "Believe it or not, the loss of money didn't really bother me. The fact that some people had taken advantage of me was the hard thing to accept. I did find out who my real friends were.

"Some of the men in the same company took bankruptcy as a way out and then moved away. One man told me, 'The only thing anyone could do for me is to put a .38 to the back of my head and shoot me.' Four of us just kept working, and we're all in good shape today. Those who took bankruptcy haven't recovered yet.

"It took me five years to recoup my losses. I learned that it isn't what happens to you that is important—it's how you react. You can always come back. Happiness is in the journey—not the destination."

I wish I had known that back in my student days when I was having such a difficult time. With the advantage of hindsight I can now look back and realize some of my mistakes....

... My first summer as a student salesman for The Southwestern Company I had done well. The next summer I recruited fifteen students from my campus and received a commission on their sales. I had the sixth best team in sales, and out of 600 I was the number-seven salesman in our division. I doubled my profits from the previous summer.

Instead of continuing to do my best, however, I became overconfident. I didn't work as hard at recruiting during the school year and took only two people to sales school the next May. I wasn't mentally prepared to start selling again.

As the summer wore on, I became discouraged. I wasn't reaching my weekly goals. I got off schedule, and though I tried hard to get back on, I just couldn't. The last two weeks I was so psyched out that I couldn't make myself knock on a door. I was so embarrassed that I called my sales manager and asked him to mail my check to school so I wouldn't have to face the people at The Southwestern Company. He persuaded me to come through Nashville anyway. I finished thirtieth in sales. In the eyes of many, that was OK, but I knew it was far below my potential. I hadn't done my best.

A real fear swept over me as to whether or not I could make a comeback the next summer and get on a good schedule. I didn't know then that the solution to my problem would have been to accept the fact that I hadn't done as well as I had expected to and go on from there. One slow season didn't mean I couldn't bounce back even stronger the next season if I'd commit myself to a set of principles that would make it possible.

I had been looking for an easier way, and when I was assured that I could get rich quicker with less effort by investing in a new cosmetic company, I'd

Principle 1: Accept Your Situation

bought it. I bought it big. Then when the pyramid operation went under, so did I.

After the scheme failed, I spent months feeling like a ship lost in a fog. I knew there had to be a way to return to solid ground, but all the signals were distorted. After three summers of selling, I was quite knowledgeable in motivation and success principles, but none of them could get me back on course, because I wasn't applying them.

It's not what you know that helps you to win—it's what you do with what you know. I could tell others how to be successful, but I couldn't break through the fog of self-pity that kept me from doing it myself.

I just didn't want to believe that the person who was really responsible for my problems was Dave Dean. I didn't want to admit to myself that I had fouled up so royally. I wanted to blame others for the shape I was in, but I knew too well I was responsible for the choices I had made.

Another reason I found it extremely difficult to be honest about my situation was that I just didn't know if I was willing to make the kind of commitment necessary to bail myself out of my problems. Finally I recognized it was either sink or swim. I couldn't continue treading water much longer.

After the phone call from Glenn Jackson, I faced my situation squarely for the first time. I totally and completely accepted my situation exactly the way it was and decided to do something about it. That acceptance was the lifeline that put me back on course. The course was certain to be stormy, but at last the fog was gone and I could start moving.

Accepting my situation freed me to commit myself

Now Is Your Time to Win

to basic success principles I knew worked. This realization, this total acceptance of my situation and the commitment to doing whatever was necessary to bounce back from failure to success, had taken only *thirty seconds.*

PRINCIPLE 2

Be Willing to Fail

As I was working up courage to enter the office of the bank president, a saying that I had repeated so often during my selling days came back to me:

> The credit belongs to the man who is actually in the arena, whose face is marred by dust and sweat and blood... who knows the great enthusiasms, the great devotions; who spends himself in a worthy cause; who at the best knows in the end the triumph of high achievement, and... if he fails, at least fails while daring greatly, so that his place shall never be with those cold and timid souls who know neither victory nor defeat.

I took a deep breath and plunged through the doorway. The broad-shouldered, efficient-looking bank executive in his pin-striped suit looked up at me quizzically from behind his massive desk.

I swallowed hard, introduced myself, and tried to

sound confident as I rattled off my well-rehearsed proposal of debt payment. Although he listened politely, he didn't seem too excited about the delay. He did appreciate my being honest with him about my financial situation, and agreed to set up a deferred monthly payment plan. The encounter hadn't been nearly as bad as I had anticipated.

A couple of weeks later, George Butler knocked on my door. George was now a sales manager with The Southwestern Company, and was doing some recruiting on campus. He talked with me about coming back to sell books the next summer. I thanked him but said, "George, I'd like to picture myself being able to do well at selling again, but I just don't know if I can. I remember when John Emery, one of my best friends, first challenged me to sell four years ago. It was a hard decision because it was straight commission with no guarantees.

"My sales experience had been limited to childhood ventures selling seeds, Christmas cards, and Mary Foelbers Butter Balls. However, I finally committed myself, followed John's suggestions, and it worked out very well. But the last two weeks of my third summer I got off schedule and couldn't even make myself knock on another door. I still don't think I've gotten over it. That was a year and a half ago. The passing of time hasn't restored my confidence toward selling. As a matter of fact, I believe the fear has been magnified. George, I guess I'm just afraid to fail."

"Dave, I know how you feel. Everybody has fears. But failure to face a fear never solves it—it only gives it time to grow. You don't have to make a decision today anyway. Think about it."

Principle 2: Be Willing to Fail

By the time George returned a few weeks later, I had realized there was a lot of truth to his words: the fear had grown.

"Dave, are you ready to make that commitment to go sell again next summer?"

"George, I really want to. You know how badly I need the money, and one of these days I need to face the fear of failure. But, I just don't know if I can produce the way I once did."

"Dave, maybe you can't."

"What?"

"I said, 'Maybe you can't,' but you're never going to know until you try. There is no disgrace in failing—the disgrace is in not trying. You've got absolutely nothing to lose and a lot to gain. Look at it this way. If selling books doesn't work out, the sun's still going to shine. And you'll still have a couple of good years left to try something else. You're making this too big a deal."

He pulled out a contract and said, "Sign this thing and let's get on with it."

"George, I believe you're right. Let me think about it for a while and I'll get back to you."

"You don't need to think about it anymore. You've thought about it too much already. David, you've got to be willing to fail. Now sign this contract." Without saying another word, I took his pen and signed the dotted line. Interestingly enough, after the commitment had been made, I felt good about it. I had taken another step.

My folks gave me $200 as a graduation gift and assured me they were behind me 100 percent. I used the money to buy a '53 Chevrolet for $125. The car was nearly as old as I was, but fortunately I was in better condition than the Chevy. I couldn't help but smile as I went putting down the highway. This wasn't quite like the new Buick Riviera I had had, but it sure beat walking as I had been doing for the last few months.

Shortly after I pulled into Nashville for the start of sales school, I ran into the previous year's number-one salesman, Dave Ditto. He said, "Aren't you Dave Dean?"

"Yes, I am."

"I've heard my older brother talk of you. You used to be pretty good, didn't you?"

"Yeah, I guess so." I decided right then that whatever Ditto's final ranking would be for the year, I was going to beat it.

At the office I ran into Dortch Oldham, then president of The Southwestern Company. "Dave, it's good to have you back with us. I hope you have a great summer. By the way, have you ever made the President's Club?"

"No, Dortch, I haven't. I've come close a couple of times, but have never hit it."

"Why not do it your first week?"

In 1970, making the President's Club meant selling two thousand dollars' worth of books in a week. At my rate of commission, that meant a profit of over eight hundred dollars for one week's work. That was quite a challenge. "Dortch, I sure will give it my best," I pledged.

The next day George Butler introduced me to Jeff Wilson and John Reed, two crackerjack salesmen, who were to be my roommates for the summer. At the close of sales school we all headed for Aiken, South Carolina, our sales locality.

Principle 2: Be Willing to Fail

At 7:59 A.M. Monday morning I was headed toward my first house. The moment of truth had arrived. Despite my preparation, I was uptight wondering if I could still sell. The first lady I demonstrated books to was nice, but didn't buy. On the way to the next house I repeated, "The credit belongs to the man who is actually in the arena...."

After a few more houses I made a sale. I was on my way. By 9:30 P.M. I had sold 480 dollars' worth of books and was tired, but elated. If I could have five more consistent days, I would hit the President's Club.

Going into Saturday, I had sold $1,750. I got off to a slow start. I couldn't give a book away. I sold my first book at 3:00 P.M. At 9:00 P.M. I was still $100 short. I started looking for lighted houses. I made more demonstrations, but no sales. So close.

At 11:15 that evening I drove by a house where several couples were out on the porch talking, so I stopped. I walked up to the house and said, "You're going to have a hard time believing this but...." I sold a set of books which clinched my entry into the prestigious President's Club, and I had actually made over eight hundred dollars in commissions.

At 1:00 A.M. I called Glenn Jackson to tell him the great news. At that hour of the morning he wasn't quite as enthusiastic as I was, but he was really proud to see that I was off to a good start.

I was thrilled when the company progress report came out with my name at the top of the list. I had been willing to fail, had faced the fear, and was conquering it.

Until that experience I used to make the mistake of looking at successful people where they were, without considering what they had gone through to get there. During a recent interview in Phoenix, Arizona, TV legend Art Linkletter told me some of his experiences. Art had spent six years "wandering around the country" trying to break into show business. He had kept talking to film directors and broadcast executives. Finally, he got his first break on "People Are Funny" which ran every Friday on NBC for nineteen years. Then one day he interviewed his four-year-old son, Jack, as a family memento. He happened to have a copy of the recording with him when he called on a San Francisco station. The interview was broadcast and the mail came pouring in.

"I saw a flag waving," Art said. "Suddenly I realized how much people are interested in kids. Here was an untapped opportunity." The result was the highly successful "House Party," which ran five days a week, fifty-two weeks a year for twenty-five years.

"Even after my first big break," Art continued, "I had a lot of failures. But each failure was only a temporary thing. You don't really fail; you just have a disappointing experience."

There's no doubt that Art Linkletter is a winner. He continues to travel thousands of miles each year, inspiring people to believe that life can be a winning experience, that they can reach their full potential by committing themselves to persist until they succeed.

Fear of failure keeps many people from committing themselves to attempt lofty goals and secret ambitions.

Mark Spitz won two gold medals in swimming in the 1968 Olympic games in Mexico City. Most athletes would have been thrilled to have won one gold medal, let alone two. Spitz, however, was extremely

Principle 2: Be Willing to Fail

disappointed because he fell two gold medals short of his goal. It would have been so much easier for him to have retired from swimming and say, "I know I could do better in the next games if I want to, but I just don't want to." That would have been safe. Or he could have said, "I'm going to come back in four years and win more medals than I did last time." That, too, would have been safe. But he told the sports world that in Munich at the next Olympics he was going to win seven gold medals, a feat that had never been accomplished in the history of Olympic competition. That's what you call "being willing to fail."

Bob Richards was speaking to The Southwestern Company's sales managers in Dallas, and said that when Mark Spitz told him he was going to win seven gold medals, he almost laughed. Even though Bob had set high goals himself and had been Decathlon Champion twice, he knew how impossible it was to win seven gold medals. He said he came close to replying, "Yeah, Mark, and my mother is going to run a 3:50 mile, too."

Mark endured four strenuous years of training and a lot of ridicule. Then the news flashed around the world from Munich, Germany, that Mark Spitz had won his seven gold medals in the 1972 Olympics.

In 1960 when Tom Landry took on the job of head coach of the newly formed Dallas Cowboys' franchise, he knew the early years would be difficult. He was right. The first season the Cowboys' scorecard read: Won 0—Lost 11—Tied 1.

It takes courage to continue to be willing to fail. Tom Landry did not have a year when his club won more games than they lost until his sixth season.

Now Is Your Time to Win

"With so many defeats, what kept you believing you could produce a winning team?" I asked him, as we talked at the Cowboys' headquarters.

"Oh, I never felt we were being defeated. I never once believed it wouldn't happen. It was just a matter of time.

"Winning and losing, Dave, is a teaching and learning experience. You beat somebody and you're teaching him something. If you get beat, then you're learning something. You just catalog all those learning experiences until you don't make the mistakes anymore. It isn't necessarily what happens to you, but how you react, and a winner has a winning attitude even in defeat."

Cheryl Prewitt Blackwood, Miss America 1980, shared with me: "When I was five years old, we had a milkman who used to tell me that someday I was going to be Miss America. I guess that planted a seed in my mind. I entered my first pageant when I was eighteen. It was a Miss America preliminary—Miss Choctaw County in Mississippi. I lost. The next year I entered the Miss Mississippi State pageant, and lost again. The following year I entered Miss Mississippi State again, and again I lost. The third year at Mississippi State, which was my fourth year in a pageant, I won the university title and thought I was finally on my way, but lost at the state level. The fifth spring I entered another local pageant and won. I then won Miss Mississippi and went on to Atlantic City and won the Miss America Pageant. But it had taken me five full years.

"The good part about winning is not winning when it is easy, but when it's difficult, when the obstacles are bigger than you can imagine, when you've

Principle 2: Be Willing to Fail

had defeats. That makes winning even greater. Because you know what it's like to go through the heartbreak before you get to win!"

Being willing to fail often means giving up security. Ron Huff started out in college to be a dentist. He switched to business, dropped out, got married, went back and graduated, directed choirs a few years, then took a secure job in an in-law's advertising agency. All the time he wanted to write music.

Several years after he was established in the business, I asked Ron how he had gotten into music full time. "Writing music had been burning hot in my mind. It wasn't an easy or a quick decision, because I had been writing music for years, but my wife, Donna, and I decided this was the time in our lives when we should step out a little farther."

The Huffs moved to Nashville with three sons, no money for furniture, and no assurance of a regular income. "I gave myself ten years to reach my goals in the music business," he said. In a few years Ron Huff became one of the top arranger/orchestrators in the country. One of his arrangements "Alleluia" has sold close to a million units. He is now president of Soundstage Studios and has worked with such stars as Dionne Warwick, The Lennon Sisters, Debbie Boone, Johnny Cash, and a host of others.

Coach Bill Hodges was willing to fail in his recruiting efforts. One of the top high school basketball players in the nation graduated and accepted a scholarship to Indiana University, instead of to Hodges' school. After a very short time there the fellow dropped out. He had come from a small town in southern Indiana and didn't feel comfortable at all at the big university.

Now Is Your Time to Win

Coach Bill Hodges, then the assistant basketball coach at Indiana State in Terre Haute, Indiana, became aware of the situation and decided to go after him and bring him to Indiana State. Coach Hodges said, "He was thinking about trying out with the pros. Physically he probably would have been able to handle that; emotionally, I didn't feel he was ready. He was right out of high school. To make the grade with the pros, you have to be strong emotionally. And since he'd left Indiana University, I was pretty sure he wasn't ready."

"Did you know him prior to that?" I asked Hodges.

"No. I went down to talk to him, but he really didn't want to talk to me. He'd had it with recruiters and college, and wasn't interested in returning.

"I finally found him with his grandmother at a Laundromat. He said flatly that he wasn't interested in talking with me.

"I told him I wasn't going to pressure him, just wanted to talk with him. His grandmother said, 'Oh, it won't hurt to talk.' So I went to his grandmother's house and we sat down and talked about an hour."

"What were his main objections?"

"He didn't appreciate the fact that when he'd left Indiana University, people had been really down on him."

"What changed his mind?"

"We got to talking about a friend of his who was a fine basketball player. They'd been playing AAU ball together in an industrial league. He said his friend could have made a great professional player if he'd gone to college. I told him, 'One of these days they're going to be saying the same thing about you.'

"I could see that really had an impact on him. I left

Principle 2: Be Willing to Fail

it there, and we didn't talk anymore that day. After five days I had all the paperwork necessary. I went back and told him I had come to take him to Indiana State to college and to play ball.

" 'How did you know I would come?' he asked.

" 'I never once doubted it.' "

This great ballplayer went to Indiana State where he redshirted his first year because of eligibility rules. Under Bill Hodges who became head coach, he went on to have an outstanding career. His senior year he took Indiana State to the final game of the NCAA playoffs. The outstanding college basketball player of the year, he was drafted by the Boston Celtics and is having quite a career. In the 1982 NBA All-Star game he was voted the Most Valuable Player. You might have heard of him. His name is Larry Byrd.

What keeps most people from realizing their potential? Mary Kay Ash put her finger on the answer beautifully.

"Fear. Fear is the root of all of it," she told me. "Fear of rejection. Fear of not succeeding. Fear of losing whatever money you might have. All the fears that we have as human beings. If there's one equal factor where women are concerned, it's a lack of self-confidence. To see a woman so timid and shy she could hardly talk over the phone develop in a few months into a beautiful, personable woman is really wonderful.

"Mary Kay Cosmetics has grown tremendously, primarily because women are terrific. They're really able to sell, especially if it's something they believe in."

Mary Kay can speak with authority on the subject

of being willing to fail. After working in direct sales for twenty-five years, she decided to write a book to help other women overcome the hurdles that she had encountered. Once her ideas were on paper, she thought, *Wouldn't it be great if somebody did this instead of just talking about it?*

"So I put my money where my mouth was and put my life savings into a cosmetic formula that I had been using the past ten years," she explained. Mary Kay Cosmetics did $34,000 in retail sales the first year—1963. In 1981 Mary Kay Cosmetics had 150,000 independent consultants and 3,000 directors with gross sales in excess of $200 million.

Let me ask you a few questions. What kind of goal would you set if you knew beyond a shadow of a doubt it was impossible to fail? Would your goal be a whole lot different from what it is now? What's keeping you from pulling out the stops and committing yourself to a goal that would really cause you to stretch?

Back in my turbulent college days I was challenged by the life of the Great Emancipator—Abraham Lincoln. I began collecting books and miscellaneous facts about him. As I learned more about him, I realized that this was a man who truly had been willing to fail:

    1831 Failed in business
    1832 Defeated for state legislature
    1833 Failed in business again
    1834 Elected to state legislature
    1835 Sweetheart died
    1836 Had nervous breakdown
    1838 Defeated for speaker of state legislature
    1840 Defeated for elector

Principle 2: Be Willing to Fail

1843 Defeated for Congress
1846 Elected to Congress
1848 Defeated for Congress
1855 Defeated for Senate
1856 Defeated for Vice-president
1858 Defeated for Senate
1860 Elected President of the United States

Lincoln's example and the stories of others who, though willing to fail, had ultimately become successes inspired me back in those dark college days, but they didn't make my fear disappear. During the eighteen months before I went back to selling books, I had the desire to conquer the fear of failing, but I couldn't pull it off. In thinking about the lives of people I considered winners, I finally realized that success is a process of setting and achieving a series of small goals that lead to the accomplishment of an ultimate goal.

I started reviewing my own progress. At my lowest ebb, it had been Ben and Carolyn Hodgin at the Pizza King who had kept me sane. Neither of them was a trained counselor, yet they had a great deal of common sense, and were concerned listeners. Then Bob Davenport gave me hope. College roommates Gary Rickner, Jim Messner, and Dan Gordon tolerated my moodiness and challenged me to do something about my situation. Southwestern salespeople—John Emery, Rick Turner, David T. Brown, and Mel and Judy Leach—continued to believe in me. Glenn Jackson demonstrated his confidence in me. It was encouraging to have friends who would stick with me in spite of my tough circumstances.

By associating with positive people like these, I

found my outlook gradually changing. Their optimism was contagious. I realized that losers tend to gravitate toward other losers because they love to remind each other that "it can't be done." These winners helped me redirect my thinking and caused me to remember I could channel my thoughts if I really wanted to.

After I had accepted my situation and had become willing to fail, I saw that continually rehashing the past was unproductive. I needed to control my thoughts, instead of letting my thoughts control me. *Controlling your thoughts is the ultimate discipline.*

Instead of being my own worst enemy, I befriended myself. I quit saying, "This can't be real" or "I'll never get out of this" or "Double D, how could you be so stupid?" That was only reinforcing negative emotions. So I started telling myself, "This, too, shall pass" and "I'm going to pay back every dollar" and "Double D, look how much you're learning at a young age."

Then I'd smile at my reflection in the mirror and count my grey hairs, which were multiplying rapidly. I found that talking positively over and over again to myself and others really helped, because it's very difficult to talk positively and think negatively at the same time. Repeating positive phrases reinforced my determination to win.

Getting back to reading good positive material was refreshing. I lived with Og Mandino's *The Greatest Salesman in the World.* I was also helped by *The Magic of Thinking Big* by Dr. David J. Schwartz, *Success through a Positive Mental Attitude* by W. Clement Stone, and *How I Raised Myself from Failure to Success in Selling*

Principle 2: Be Willing to Fail

by Frank Bettger. I also found the Bible to be a genuine source of inspiration.

I underlined passages in these books, studied them, memorized portions, and meditated on them until finally I realized it was possible to so saturate myself with information about being willing to fail that it could become a means of procrastination. It's easy, even enjoyable, to talk, to think, to read about being willing to fail, but to actually do it, you've got to take definite action. It took George Butler, a man who knew me and my situation, to help me make a decision on a plan of action I knew was right. I was thankful he did. People will do anything to procrastinate, putting themselves back on the line once they have failed.

That sounds as if signing that dotted line solved all my problems. But if I'm going to be honest, I've got to make a confession. When I finally walked up to that first door, after eighteen months of not being able to make myself knock on a door, I was still afraid. I feared both failure and rejection. The fear didn't leave me, but I knocked on that door in spite of it.

While waiting for the customer to answer the door, I muttered to myself, "The credit belongs to the man who is actually in the arena, whose face is marred by dust and sweat and blood... who knows the great enthusiasms, the great devotions; who spends himself in a worthy cause...."

PRINCIPLE 3

Make Daily Preparations

Making the President's Club that first week gave me a tremendous boost. The second week was another strong week. The third week was also good. The fourth week I hit the President's Club again, and was averaging $800 a week in commissions. I was beginning to believe that this could be my best summer ever if I could keep doing the little things that made the difference. Neglecting those "little things" had caused my downfall back in the summer of '68.

Before starting the critical summer of '70, I vowed to go back to the basics. What I learned from the mistakes of the past was that if you neglect the little things, you'll ultimately fail in the big things. Daily preparation kept me from neglecting the little things.

Repeating the Serenity Prayer became part of my daily mental preparation: "God, grant me the serenity to accept the things I can't change, the courage to change the things I can, and the wisdom to know the difference."

That helped me keep in perspective what I could

and could not change. I couldn't change the weather, the economy, or the attitudes of other people. I couldn't control when and who would buy. I could control my work and sleep habits. I could control my attitude and my thinking. I could control being prepared for the day. And I could control the number of calls and presentations I made each day.

With the assumption that daily preparation begins the evening before, I did my paperwork each night instead of waiting until morning. Before hitting the sack, I'd decide exactly where I would start knocking on doors the next day.

For me half the battle was getting my body to a vertical position. As an incentive to jump out of bed each morning, my roommates, John Reed and Jeff Wilson, and I would nightly put money in the middle of the floor an equal distance from each bed. When the alarm went off, the first one to reach it got to keep it. There were a few mid-air collisions but no casualties. At 6:00 A.M. I'd be in a cold shower, singing, "It's a grand thing to be a book man...."

Then while shaving, I'd tell the man in the mirror: "This is the best day I've ever had. I can, I will, I'm going to help thirty people a day live a richer, fuller, more meaningful life because I stopped by and showed them my books. And I can, I will, I'm going to become, by the grace of God, day by day the greatest salesman The Southwestern Company has ever had."

While dressing and getting ready, I would listen to an inspirational tape. During breakfast, which usually consisted of a deluxe cheeseburger with a fried egg in the middle, french fries, and a chocolate milkshake, I'd look over my sales talks and read a "scroll"

Principle 3: Make Daily Preparations

from Og Mandino's *The Greatest Salesman in the World*.

Before leaving for the sales locality, I'd mentally prepare myself for anything that could happen that day. *This may be a $200 commission day; it may be a $20 commission day. A $200 day isn't going to make my summer, and a $20 day won't break it,* I'd remind myself. *I may make several calls where I don't even get inside. I may make several presentations that I don't sell. I may hit a stretch where a lot of people aren't home. Some people may be in a bad mood.*

It may rain. I may get another flat tire. I may have mechanical trouble. I may have some times when I don't like what I'm going through.

By being mentally prepared for anything, I was seldom surprised. I expected the best, but was prepared for the "what if's" and had already determined how I would handle each one. If I was selling like crazy, fine; if not, I knew it would only be temporary.

I believed in the law of averages. I had the confidence that if I would consistently work hard 12-1/2 to 13-1/2 hours a day and make between twenty-five and thirty good presentations daily, then the law of averages would not fail me.

My sample case would be at the first door at 7:59 A.M. My goal would be to make at least twenty-five demonstrations a day. Each demonstration would take approximately twenty minutes, making between twenty-five and thirty demonstrations in a day possible, but I had to hustle. I would aim for ten demonstrations between 8:00 and 12:30, ten between 12:30 and 5:00, and ten more between 5:00 and 9:30 P.M.

This routine would get tiresome at times, but my goal for the summer was high, and I had learned the hard way the importance of staying on schedule. *Suc-*

cess is not a matter of chance—it's a matter of choices. Success isn't something you hope happens. It is high achievement accomplished by consistent daily preparation and commitment to a goal with a daily plan of action.

Accepting my situation, being willing to fail, and making daily preparations were three of the seven principles I used that summer to turn my life around. The *thirty seconds* in which I had faced my situation honestly and had made the commitment to do whatever needed to be done had redirected my thinking, changed my attitude, and started me back on the road to success. However, the debt still loomed over my head. Being willing to fail had meant a three-month commitment to selling books, an opportunity that could start me chipping away at my monumental millstone. I felt certain that the more diligently I applied the rest of the principles, the larger the chips would be.

This habit of making daily preparations is a common characteristic of many of the winners I've talked with in the years since.

John Naber, an Olympic champion, shared with me how he learned this principle at an early age. In high school he would swim daily from 5:00 A.M. to 7:30 A.M. and from 4:00 P.M. to 6:00 P.M. Every other day he spent thirty minutes lifting weights. How does a young man keep at such a schedule? "I wanted to go to the Olympics," he explained. "There are over one hundred thousand amateur athletes in swim training. They spend four hours a day, six days a week, eleven months a year, ten miles a day, up and down the pool.

Principle 3: Make Daily Preparations

"That doesn't sound very exciting, but we try to motivate each other to keep plugging away," he stressed. "Anyone who goes to the Olympic trials has given much of his life to the sport. Only a small percentage will make the team.

"In swimming you are basically racing against the clock. I'd try to improve myself .01 or .001 of a second each time. In four years I went from 59.5 to 55.5. I'd cut that up into amounts of .3 of a second or .12 of a second a day. I'd be racing the clock, but I'd also play mind games. I'd imagine the cheer of the crowd and the feel of the cold chain of the gold medal being slipped over my head."

That kind of consistent daily preparation was phenomenal, but John had a goal. At age twenty he had made it to the 1976 Olympics in Montreal where the years of daily discipline finally paid off. He won four gold medals. Consistent daily preparation pays big dividends for those who make this principle a habit.

Spencer Hays also learned the principle of daily preparation early in life. He had been raised in the small town of Gainesville, Texas, and clearly remembers working hard from the time he was twelve years old to help support his family. He had earned a basketball scholarship to Texas Christian University, and it was during his freshman year there that he first heard about a summer opportunity to sell books published by a company in Nashville called *The Southwestern Company*.

So in the spring of 1956 he borrowed forty dollars from his grandmother Mary Moore, put his new bride, Marlene, and their clothes into his car, and drove to Tennessee. He spent his honeymoon learning how to sell books. That was the beginning of several successful summers of selling, recruiting, and managing, and in 1960 he became a district sales manager with The Southwestern Company.

In his eleven years as a sales manager, he had built large, productive sales organizations, many years managing over 500 student salespeople at a time. In 1971, Spencer was given the responsibility for sales for the entire company. He was named president of The Southwestern Company in 1973.

Now a quarter of a century after picking up that first sample case, he is married to the same sweetheart, is chairman of the board of The Southwestern Company, and owns several other companies that in 1981 produced approximately $60 million in sales.

Spencer loves to sell. I often hear him say, "The profession of selling is the greatest profession in the world."

Spencer Hays believes in planning. "I really believe in priority lists. Each day I write down what my objectives are for that day and what I need to get done this week, next week, and even the next six months, and then I make sure I am working with a definite plan in mind. So many people spend 90 percent of their time on things that produce only 10 percent results. They confuse activity with results.

"That's why salespeople have so much to teach other people. A successful salesperson understands the value of organizing his day and knowing exactly where he's going to be each minute of that day. So many people have their days filled up with whatever happens to come along instead of saying, 'I've got to get these things done.'

"You have to have a plan, Dave. You have to be

Principle 3: Make Daily Preparations

specific about the things you are going to do to reach your goal. You have to put pressure on yourself. If you are unwilling to do the things that cause you to excel and succeed today, they won't be any easier to do tomorrow or the next day. Today is the day, and now is the time."

Spencer Hays believes in utilizing spare moments during the day: "When I am on an airplane or have to wait for something, I use the time to dictate, read, or often I pull out one of the pieces of paper I always carry with me and memorize the quotes on them—ideas that reinforce my goals. Things like, 'The man who says it can't be done is often interrupted by the man doing it' and 'Consider the postage stamp—its usefulness consists primarily in its ability to stick with one thing until it gets it done' and 'There is no philosophy by which a man can do things he thinks he can't.'

"Probably few of these quotes are originals. I read them somewhere. But you don't get credit for reading them. You don't get credit for underlining them. You only get the credit if you take them and use them. I memorize them until they become a part of me.

"Sometimes emergencies may arise that take priority over everything else you had planned for the day. So you have to change your priority list for that one day, but some people use that as an excuse for never laying out a detailed schedule and plan. You see, *failures don't plan to fail—they just fail to plan.*"

During a recruiting trip I boarded a plane in Spokane, Washington. Walking through the aisle, I stopped temporarily right in front of a lady bearing a close resemblance to "Dear Abby." I looked at her as if to say, "Are you? . . ." She took the question out of

Now Is Your Time to Win

my mouth before I could utter it and said, "Yes, I am and you're welcome to join me."

During the hour flight she shared thoughts on how she has managed to do a daily column for so many years: "You have to be organized and use your time wisely each day when you're constantly faced with deadlines." The stack of mail she had been reading emphasized her words. Abigail Van Buren is definitely a lady who has formed the habit of daily preparation.

Mort Utley, one of the nation's outstanding motivational speakers, has been delivering the closing address for each week of our sales school for twenty-five years. I've heard that speech myself at least thirty times, yet each time I find myself captivated all over again.

"How can you deliver the same speech over and over like that and still make it sound fresh?" I asked Mort.

"Preparation, Dave. I've given that speech probably five hundred times. I used to do it twenty times a week, yet I still listen to it on a tape a minimum of three times during the week before I give it. I also listen to it once or twice early in the morning before I go to the auditorium to speak. That way I know every word I'm going to say, when I'm going to say it, and how. It's just like a baseball pitcher warming up before every game."

One of Mort's favorite stories on the importance of daily preparation comes from his forty-three years of experience in the life-insurance business:

> There was a man who was failing so miserably in the business that he was about to quit.

Principle 3: Make Daily Preparations

His wife knew he had potential, but had watched him wake up morning after morning with no appointments lined up and no definite ideas about how to get started. Finally she said, "OK, if you're going to quit, that's fine, but at least give yourself a fair chance. Before going to bed, write down ten prospects you would like to sell life insurance to. Then call them and try to get appointments with a few of them." He did and got lined up with three. When he woke up the next morning, he was excited. He had a plan and already had lined up people he would see.

One prospect he called on had just left. His partner was there, however, and suggested that as long as the man had driven that far, he might as well call on the new young businessman in the store three doors down the street. The man said he had a little time, so he did and proceeded to sell the newcomer a good-sized policy. The salesman went home at the end of the day excited and feeling successful. He made a vow to himself that in the future he would do his planning the night before, and would always call on the man next door. He went on to do well in the life-insurance business and called his plan "The night before and the man next door."

A man who practices what he preaches, Mort, years ago, went to a print shop and had some sheets printed up to use in writing out his plans for the week. "I carry Last Week, This Week, and Next Week with me when I travel," he explained. "That way I know where I've been, where I am, and where I'm going. I never consider a day closed until I've written down everything I'm going to do the next day. Dave, developing this one habit could revolutionize many careers."

This habit helped Mort accomplish a great feat within the life-insurance industry. When he went with the Penn Mutual Life Insurance Company's San Francisco agency as director of training, he set a goal to make it the top-producing agency in the company. At the end of twelve years not only had he reached this goal, but also the agency had produced more ordinary life insurance than any other agency in the United States.

"Forming the habit of daily preparation should be a goal of every success-oriented individual," Mort stated. "Good habits unlock the doors to success. Losers *let* things happen; they're merely creatures of circumstances. Winners *make* things happen; they're creators of circumstances."

If anyone knows the importance of daily preparation for reaching long-range goals, it is the marathon runner. Bill Rogers has won thirty-five marathons, and held the American marathon record for six years. He also holds the record for the one-hour run and a host of others.

"You have to have goals," Bill assured me. "I started running at age fifteen back in 1963, with the Newington, Connecticut, recreation program. At the end of the summer we had a track meet, and I ran the mile race in five minutes and twenty seconds and

Principle 3: Make Daily Preparations

won the event. The following fall I joined the cross-country team as a sophomore, and I ran all through high school and college.

"I didn't enter my first marathon until I'd been running ten years. In the ten years since, I've averaged about 120 to 125 miles a week. You have to do that day by day—about twenty miles a day. It takes months and even years before you start running the marathons. You learn to run longer and longer distances, on a very gradual basis. Month by month. Year by year. I'm always running in preparation for the next race."

Consistent daily preparation pays big dividends. I asked Cheryl Prewitt Blackwood, Miss America 1980, about the competition in Atlantic City.

"If I had gone to Atlantic City and not been prepared, it would have been a tough week, because there were fifty young ladies there who wanted to be Miss America. But nobody worked harder than I had, and nobody wanted to be Miss America more than I did. For six straight weeks before the pageant, I worked from 8:00 in the morning until almost midnight every day. I spent five hours a day exercising. The swimsuit contest had always been my weakest point, but I won it in Atlantic City—and I needed those points to win the title."

Cheryl continues to prepare to win in her multifaceted career. She has authored her first book, *A Bright-Shining Place,* by Doubleday. She sings, writes songs, and has released an album with Impact Records, "I'm a Miracle." She also speaks, models, emcees beauty pageants, makes commercials, and has made a pilot for a possible TV series.

Now Is Your Time to Win

I asked real-estate entrepreneur Jim Moore what he considered one of the major characteristics of his steady successful climb. "Dave, I have formed the habit of planning my work and working my plan," he replied. "It sounds simplistic because it is, but it works. So few people do this on a consistent basis."

I had seen a firsthand example of that when I'd first met Jim in 1967. He had recruited a twenty-man team and had brought them to Nashville. I had fifteen in my team, and all of us were staying at the same motel. Glenn Jackson and other sales managers had been making a big deal about the team that managed to sit on the front row each day. On Thursday one of the sales managers said, "It's obvious Jim Moore's team is going to do well this summer—this is the fourth day in a row Jim and his men have been on the front row."

That did it. We had only one day left, so after sales school that day I called our team together, and we laid out a strategy to be on the front row on closing day. "After all, it's not how you start a race that people remember," I preached at them. "It's how you finish that counts."

We knew Jim would also be going for a clean sweep on the fifth day, so we decided not to take any chances. We divided into shifts of two men each and at midnight started stationing men outside the main entrance of the small building where sales school was being held.

About 7:00 A.M. I finished my shift and went back to the room to shower. I felt tired, but proud because I knew we were about to upset the great Jim Moore team.

At 7:30 A.M. one of my men came running in

Principle 3: Make Daily Preparations

shouting, "Dave, Jim's team is sitting on the front row!"

"What?" I exclaimed. "That's impossible! The doors aren't even open yet."

"Yeah, but at 7:30 A.M. Jim Moore and his men came charging toward us at the front door. Then just before they reached us, they pivoted around and ran to the side entrance. Just like in a James Bond movie, a door opened out of nowhere, and a janitor let them in. Then the door was slammed shut. They waved to us through the glass doors as they walked triumphantly to the front row."

Jim told me later that they thought our team might possibly make a play for the honored seats, so he had planned ahead. He got the janitor's phone number, called him, and paid him to come in early and be at the side door right at 7:30 A.M. to pull off the caper.

Even though I was upset, I couldn't help but respect the extra preparation and determination that have been so characteristic of Jim's career.

Jim started selling books in 1966. Jim was in the top twenty of all first-year salesmen his first summer and saved over $4,000. His twenty-man team from Southern Methodist University in '67 finished number one in The Southwestern Company. He then had the number-one team in the company five years back to back. Jim's last year to sell, he set records that still stand. He was the number-one experienced salesman of the 958 he had competed with. He was also the number-one student manager out of 207 managers, and had managed the number-one first-year salesmen. He also had the number-one organization in The Southwestern Company. His total commissions were over $50,000.

Now Is Your Time to Win

Jim went into the real-estate business in 1972. He had a couple of slow years during the recession, but stuck it out. For the next several years Jim made steady progress. Then during an eighteen-month period of time between 1979 and 1980, he sold 43 million dollars' worth of commercial property, being one of the very top—if not the top—real-estate salesmen in Dallas, Texas. During that time, Jim formed his own company, Moore-Myers and Associates, which in 1981 had a net worth of $12 million.

Jim continues to prepare daily. He realizes there are two kinds of people in this world—those who look for a way and those who look for an excuse.

An illustration sticks in my mind on the long-term rewards for consistent daily preparation and effort. It was told to me by motivational speaker Zig Ziglar, who, in turn, heard it from Joel Weldon, a professional speaker. As we taxied to the airport in New Orleans, he said, "The Chinese bamboo tree is a remarkable tree, Dave. The Chinese plant the seed for the tree, water it, fertilize it, but the first year nothing happens. Then the second year they continue watering and fertilizing it, but still nothing. The third year nothing. The fourth year they continue to water and fertilize it, with no evident results. Then during the fifth year, in six weeks the Chinese bamboo tree grows ninety feet. But it didn't take six weeks to grow ninety feet. If during any of those years they hadn't watered and fertilized the seed daily, there would have been no Chinese bamboo tree."

That story struck a responsive chord in me, for the same patience and persistence necessary for the growth of the Chinese bamboo tree would also be necessary for the daily preparation it takes to keep on

Principle 3: Make Daily Preparations

schedule to win. After I'd accepted my situation and become willing to fail, it had been that same kind of daily persistence that had gotten me off to a good start during the summer of 1970. It was also a key ingredient toward producing the mental attitude that prepared me for the development of the next principle in my quest for success.

PRINCIPLE 4

Be a Professional

After I'd been a month on the field, my sales were moving in a positive direction. I'd read that the secret of success was in deliberately forming good habits. I had formed the habit of staying on a good schedule. Getting up at the same time, working 12-1/2 to 13-1/2 hours a day, and making the calls necessary to make my daily goal in demonstrations were paying off.

My roommates John Reed and Jeff Wilson were from other universities, and had been total strangers to me before the summer. We'd become close friends in spite of the intense competition among us. They were good schedule men—positive, highly motivated, great salesmen, and a lot of fun to be with. Jeff and John were just the right combination for me that crucial summer.

When I said the competition was intense, I wasn't exaggerating, but that was great because it kept the pressure on me to produce at maximum efficiency. Our trio was quickly becoming the top-producing "headquarters" in the whole company. At the end of

Now Is Your Time to Win

the sixth week all three of us were ranked in the top fifteen in The Southwestern Company in total production to date, with Jeff and John running slightly ahead of me. Since we had all hit the President's Club at different weeks, George Butler, our sales manager, challenged us all to hit the Club in the same week. He promised to run a special write-up in the company report if we made it—pictures and all. That was all we needed. We were all egotistical enough to feel that was a worthwhile goal.

By Friday morning, Jeff was sitting on $1,400, and right on schedule. John had sold $1,200 and needed two $400 days to do it. I was sitting on $1,100 and knew that somehow I was going to have to sell $900 more of books the next two days. Friday night, Jeff was up to $1,700 and was right on schedule. John had sold $400, putting him at $1,600. I knew they were both going to go over. Friday I had worked hard and given it my best shot, but had only managed to sell $200 and was sitting on $1,300.

At breakfast Saturday morning, I was rather depressed because I felt I had let my comrades down. I knew they were getting ready to hit the President's Club, but I didn't see any way I could make it. The most I'd ever sold in one day was $550. John and Jeff had each had a $600-plus day, but none of us had approached $700. It would take a miracle for me to sell $700 on the day that would put our team into the limelight. John Reed, in his typically confident attitude, said, "Well, gosh, Dean, it's only $700. You can do that. Just go do it."

I thought to myself, *Only $700!* Instead I replied, "Well, John, maybe you're right. I'll go for it."

Because of car trouble, I got started later than

Principle 4: Be a Professional

usual. As I headed my Chevy toward the little town of Washington, Georgia, where we were now selling, I kept thinking to myself, *Only $700! Well, Double D, you've got nothing to lose. Let's give it a shot.* I figured I needed to sell $233.33 every four-and-a-half hours. Even as I wrote the figure on my "crystalized goal sheet," it seemed impossible.

At 10:00 A.M. I sold a fifty dollar set. I knew that if I was going to have a chance at that $700 figure, I would have to sell sets most of the day. Single books for $32.95 just wouldn't add up fast enough.

I'd been working the area around the town for a week and had sold books to quite a few of the leading people. I had some great names to use as testimonials —the mayor, one of the leading dentists, a lawyer, and the chief of police had all bought from me. Those names would have helped, but it seemed the whole town was gone to Little League Day at the park. Few people were home. By 3:00 P.M. I had sold only 125 dollars' worth of books. Selling another $575 in the next six-and-a-half hours didn't seem very promising.

I thought, *Maybe I'll get better results in another area,* so I drove toward greener pastures. I don't know why, but for some reason whenever I wasn't selling well, I'd start thinking that any other sales locality would have better prospects than mine. I was about two miles outside the city limits when I thought to myself, *David, what in the world are you doing? Here it is 3:00 P.M. Saturday afternoon, and you're getting ready to drive fifteen or twenty miles and start knocking on doors in a brand-new county with no names. You can't sell the amount of books you need to that way. At least you have good names to use in Washington, and you have a chance if you just*

63

head the car back into town and move as fast as you possibly can.

I made a U-turn and drove right back to the house where I had left off. The family had just returned from the ballgame and proceeded to buy a sixty dollar set. I walked next door and sold another sixty dollar set. Two doors down, I sold a seventy dollar set. At 5:00 I sold a thirty-five dollar book. I went out to the car and added up my totals and found I was right at $350. I still had $350 to go, but I had a strange feeling that somehow, someway, I was about to accomplish the impossible.

I'd heard the expression all my life, "When you're hot, you're hot, and when you're not, you're not." Well, I was sizzling. I moved faster than I ever had. I sold my next three customers and suddenly it seemed I was invincible. I was so excited about the possibility of hitting my goal that I felt like walking into homes and saying, "Hi, Mrs. Jones, my name is Dave Dean. Would you like to take a look at what you're about to buy?" I didn't really say that, but my positive attitude sure helped.

I sold a big set, then another one, then yet another one, and at 9:15 I needed only fifty dollars to accomplish my seemingly unattainable goal. At exactly 9:45, I made the sale that put me over the $700 figure. I walked casually back to the car, drove out of hearing distance, and let out a triumphant yell. I had done it.

As I drove back toward the restaurant where Jeff, John, and I met each night, I was probably more excited and thrilled than at any point in my life. I had never shot for a goal that high. I felt as if I had just broken a four-minute mile or had won a gold medal.

As I strolled into the restaurant, I decided to play

Principle 4: Be a Professional

it cool and not mention hitting my goal. I sat down and John looked right at me and said, "You did it, didn't you, Dean?"

"Did what?" I asked innocently.

"You hit $700, didn't you?"

"Yeah, I did, but how in the world did you know?"

"I don't know," he grinned. "I just had this strange feeling that you were going to do it."

All three of us had hit $2,000 the same week and were in the President's Club. We celebrated over steaks, basking in the glory of our victory, anticipating that big write-up in The Southwestern Company's progress report.

At the weekend sales meeting following the great achievement, I was asked what I thought was making the big difference in my summer. After thinking about it awhile, I realized that I was looking at myself and my work, that I was performing more professionally than I ever had before. Up to that summer, I had always let myself fluctuate too much. I would let my feelings get the best of me and wouldn't perform consistently. Before, if I was excited, I would really do well, but if not, my performance suffered dramatically. This summer I had made up my mind to pace myself like a good athlete on a cross-country course instead of burning out after the 100-yard dash.

I shared with the other salespeople the mental gymnastics I went through to prepare myself emotionally: "The attitude I take as I walk up to the door is if I get in—fine. If not, no big deal. If I sell, I don't get overly excited, and if I don't sell, I don't get utterly depressed. I just say, 'Thank you, Mrs. Jones, I really appreciate your time. The folks next door, would they be home?' and proceed to get a little pre-approach information about the next customer and move.

"At the next house, if I get in, fine. If not, no big deal. If I sell, I don't get overly excited. If I don't sell, I don't get utterly depressed. I just continue the routine over and over."

They didn't seem overly impressed with the secret of my success. I think some of them were looking for a magic key. Just being consistent didn't sound exciting enough, yet that was what was working for me. Maintaining a consistently professional attitude became a principle that I applied throughout the summer. I was beginning to realize that professionals pace themselves and develop the habit of performing regardless of how they feel.

That was one of the greatest lessons I learned while selling books. I didn't always feel "healthy, happy, and terrific" or feel like knocking on doors, but I found that if I could discipline myself to get started each morning, the battle was half won.

Over the years I've come to realize just how valuable that sales training has been to me. Most people are involved in some kind of selling situation every day. When a teacher presents an idea; when a doctor tries to explain to a reluctant patient why surgery is necessary; when a mother is teaching a principle of good behavior to her child; when a lawyer is presenting a case to a jury; when a coach is motivating a group of players; when an engineer is justifying a new project; when a nervous sixteen-year-old is asking a girl for a date—all of these situations involve *selling*.

Selling is really nothing more than "motivating someone else to act positively on an idea you have

Principle 4: Be a Professional

presented." Different studies have shown that only 15 percent of an individual's overall success will be directly related to the technical knowledge he has of his field. Eighty-five percent of his success will be directly related to his ability to work with and through people. The skill of communicating well to sell specific ideas is vitally important.

I asked "Dear Abby" what she considered to be one of the biggest problems in our country today, and without hesitation she replied, "Communication. If people could just talk out what's really on their minds, a lot of the problems could be solved long before they pass the point of no return."

We receive letters almost daily at The Southwestern Company from successful alumni of our program, people who are excelling in virtually every profession. Many of them attribute a great deal of their success to the principles and training they received while selling The Southwestern Company books.

Tom McDow is a great example. In 1975, Tom set a goal of building one of the top fund-raising companies in America. As president of the newly founded Nashville Educational Marketing Services, Tom started out with thirteen sales representatives and did 800,000 dollars' worth of business the first year.

During the past seven years, the company has averaged a remarkable compounded growth rate of 55 percent a year, and is continuing to grow at the same rate. Now having 165 full-time salespeople, it is on schedule to become the top fund-raising company in the country.

I asked Tom why he felt the company has grown at such a rate.

Now Is Your Time to Win

"I believed it was possible," Tom told me. "To recruit a sales organization in the beginning, I had to sell the idea that it was possible. We had no statistics to impress anyone and no sales record, so I had to sell belief. I'm sure thankful for my sales training, because even as president, I am constantly having to sell ideas on a daily basis."

"I can see where you've utilized some of the principles you learned selling books," I mused. "You had to accept the situation that you were in a brand-new business with no past record to use in recruiting."

"I sure did," he laughed. "Someone suggested that I fake it until I make it. That's pretty much what I did at first."

"Did you have a fear of failure?"

"I certainly did. Fear of failure isn't all bad, though. It kept me working intensely."

"What about daily planning?"

"As the company grew, I saw an even greater need for planning. I had to take time to think, plan ahead, and look at the overall perspective. Each Sunday night I made a list of the things I wanted to accomplish in the coming week. Then I ranked them one, two, and three according to how that activity would pay off. Next I ranked them *A*, *B*, and *C* according to priority. I picked out all the *A*-ones and fitted them into the weekly schedule. As I had time, I worked in the *B*-twos. *C*-threes I delegated to someone else."

"From your experience, what do you think makes a real professional?"

"That's tough to put your finger on. I do know that most people don't really know what they want out of life. They just drift along. If we know what we really want, we can channel our energies toward

Principle 4: Be a Professional

reaching that goal. A professional knows what he wants, and is willing to discipline himself to make the choices and the sacrifices, if need be, to accomplish that goal. It's impossible to achieve a goal unless you have a definite picture of it in your mind. Only then can you work to make that image a reality."

"What are some practical principles that you have found helpful?"

"Every day each of us is faced with many decisions. Several times a day I ask myself, *Is what I'm doing right now the single most important thing I should be doing in relation to my goals?* Because I know that if I can make decisions on what I should do—even if at times I don't like it—then in the long run when I've accomplished the goals I've set, I'll be glad I did.

"People who have really excelled are extremely result-oriented and have formed the habit of making decisions on the basis of pleasing results, not just pleasing activities. It's not what you do or how much you do. It's what you get done that counts.

"One of the greatest thrills and joys in life is that of achieving and accomplishing worthwhile goals. It's like the great Vince Lombardi said, 'I believe that man's greatest hour, in fact—his greatest fulfillment, his finest fulfillment, is that moment when he has worked his heart out and for a good cause lies exhausted but victorious on the field of battle—whenever, wherever that field of battle may be—in your business, in my business, or wherever.'"

Jim McEachern is another man who learned the principles of success while he was working as a book man. Now Jim is president of one of America's finest clothiers—Tom James Company. Tom James has a fine group of professionals that sell tailor-made clothing to executives in the convenience of their homes or offices. It is a rather new concept. Tom James was founded in 1966, and in the first calendar year, total sales were approximately $190,000. Jim explained, "As one of the company's first salesmen, I started talking about Tom James becoming a $100 million company as far back as 1967. Many people were skeptical that it could ever happen.

"After becoming president of Tom James in January, 1973, I clung to that vision, made a commitment to the $100 million goal, continued to prepare, and took action. I knew it would take awhile, so we set the short-range goal of doubling our production every two years. Now we'll do $30 million in sales in 1982, and are right on schedule for that $100 million mark." Tom James is now the fastest-growing men's clothing company in the United States.

Dentists Mike Buehler and Mark Gravbrot sold books for six summers and built large sales organizations before they graduated from dental school. They decided to set up a practice in Yakima, Washington, even though there were already fifty dentists in the town of 50,000 people. "We set a goal to have the city's largest dental practice," they said. "It was a big goal, but we had a plan of action. We called on every single dentist and sold ourselves well enough to get referrals from most of them. At the end of two years we had the second largest practice in Yakima, and at the end of six years, the largest. We started off with two chairs and one assistant, and by 1982, we had ten chairs and fifteen assistants, and are on schedule to do a million dollars' worth of dental work."

These former book men were able to fulfill their

Principle 4: Be a Professional

dreams because they were well trained, set specific goals, and are very professional in their work.

One of the most interesting interviews I've ever done was with a man who has seen the fulfillment of a childhood dream. He walked on the moon.

"My mother used to tell me, 'Son, that's foolishness. Don't waste your time thinking about it.'" Colonel Jim Irwin, author of *To Rule the Night,* now recalls. "I joined the Air Force and became a test pilot to qualify for the astronaut program. It took many years and many disappointments, but my third formal application was accepted."

"So you knew what you wanted to accomplish with your life and you worked toward that goal?" I asked him.

"Yes, but that was only the beginning. After I was accepted into the program, I spent another year in formal training. Lots of classroom work. Then I was assigned to the lunar module, and spent more time working with the factory that produced the vehicle. And I did a lot of testing.

"I had to develop new flying skills at the Navy's helicopter school down in Pensacola, Florida, because the lunar module is a hovercraft.

"Next I was trained as a geologist. I had to be a pretty good field observer so I would feel at home when we got to the moon. It took about five years more training.

"It's hard work, but you get caught up in the enthusiasm. Your single goal is somehow to reach the moon. To fly in space! We all felt this was the most important thing we could do with our lives, and we were willing to give our lives if that was required. We realized there was some risk, a chance we might not come back. But we had faith in ourselves, in the hardware, and in the people we were working with. The closer it came to the flight itself, the more I prayed.

"After lift-off as we saw the earth getting smaller and smaller, we came to appreciate it more. We were gone for twelve days. When we reached the moon, we decided we could do our best job on the surface if we were well rested. So after landing, we opened the top hatch, took some pictures, then climbed back in and bedded down for the night. We were pretty excited when we first landed, but we tried to approach this in a very calm and relaxed manner.

"The next morning as I squeezed out in my space suit, I tripped and stumbled. I thought, *Here the whole world is watching Jim Irwin make his grand entrance—and I'm going to land on my backside!* I reached out and grabbed a rung of the ladder and sailed out of the view of the television camera, and in so doing my attention was drawn directly overhead—and there was Earth! Just the size of a little blue marble. I said, 'Lord, I'm on the moon! I've made it.'

"It had taken almost a lifetime of preparation—twenty years. For twenty years I'd been preparing for that moment, and it was worth it all. It was worth every bit of the effort."

Jim Irwin accomplished his goal because he had a plan and a commitment to that plan. This principle was reiterated to me by one of the top country-music stars of all time—Loretta Lynn. While talking with Loretta, I asked her why she felt she had been able to accomplish what she had. She smiled and without hesitation said, "Hard work! I've worked extremely hard, and I am still doing that. I've only taken one

Principle 4: Be a Professional

day off since Christmas. But I also had a plan and a strategy that have given direction to my career." Loretta Lynn didn't become a pro by reaching the top; she reached the top because she had a professional approach toward her career from the beginning.

Tom Landry stated, "During football season I work seventeen hours a day, seven days a week." No one makes him do that. He decided long ago he was going to excel as a professional football coach. That doesn't mean you have to work seventeen hours a day to be successful, but it does mean that if you are going to excel, there is a price to pay. There are no shortcuts to the top.

One evening I was talking to Hollywood actor Dean Jones and his wife, Lori, in their San Fernando Valley home. Dean mentioned the 100,000 hopefuls in Hollywood, trying to make it as actors. "There is more to it than most people think," he assured me. "You don't just blow into Tinseltown and get your name in lights. My first job was at Knotts' Berry Farm where I did four shows a day for thirty dollars a week. Later I was able to hook on with MGM and did a few minor parts. I tried Broadway where I worked with Jane Fonda in her first play. I thought the play was my big break, but it ran only three weeks.

"Then I wasn't able to find any work for an entire year, and I got pretty hungry, sometimes literally, but I felt my future was in acting, so I just stuck with it." Dean didn't quit. He persisted and went on to star in ten Walt Disney movies including *Love Bug,* which had one of the ten highest box-office draws in its decade. He is now starring in a weekly CBS-TV series, "Herbie, The Love Bug."

There is a lot to be said for people who hang in

there month after month, year after year, as they continue to learn the skills of the trade. More times than not, people who are at the top of their professions have paid their dues to get there and stay there. I was jogging with Zig Ziglar awhile back in Phoenix, Arizona, and he mentioned that running was a very important part of his day.

"I'm an avid jogger. Keeping in shape physically helps me stay alert mentally. I do some of my most creative thinking while running."

"Zig, how did you earn the credentials to merit $5,000 a speech?" I asked.

"Dave, I was starving to death as a salesman. A speaker named P. C. Merrell persuaded me I could do things with my life I had never before dreamed possible. I went on to do well in sales and management, and then I decided I wanted to be a motivational speaker.

"I made literally thousands of speeches in my own mind, before I ever spoke from a platform. Then I spoke at every opportunity—to garden clubs, Lions, Rotaries, any place, any time I could get two or three people who would hear me. Sometimes I wondered if it was ever going to happen, but it was worth every bit of effort and sacrifice.

"It took ten years and three thousand speeches before I got my first check for a speech."

Ten years and three thousand speeches. That persistence and professionalism are why you see Zig Ziglar at the top.

I was talking to Harmon Killibrew, one of the greatest home-run hitters in the history of baseball, at a sports banquet in Yakima, Washington. He said he believed one of the greatest professionals he'd

Principle 4: Be a Professional

ever known was a man by the name of Lou Brissi. He went on to share the story.

"Brissi had just started his baseball career at age nineteen when World War II broke out, and he was drafted. During a beach assault in Sicily he was hit in the leg by enemy shrapnel. Overhearing the medics discussing amputation, he begged them to try to save the limb. 'I'm a professional baseball pitcher. If you take my leg, my career's over.'

"Fifty-six operations later Lou reported to the Philadelphia Athletics. Manager Connie Mack said sympathetically, 'Lou, I don't know if you can make the team, but we'll give you a chance.' Lou took his wind-up a little differently, but he could still get the ball over the plate. He made the team.

"His first time out he pitched against the Boston Red Socks. After he'd struck out the first two batters, Ted Williams came to the plate. Brissi got two strikes on him before Ted smashed a line drive up the middle.

"That was one of the hardest hit balls I'd ever seen!" Killibrew recalled. "The ball struck Lou on his bad leg, knocking him off his feet. A hush fell over the crowd. Connie Mack came running out to the mound.

"Lou looked up and pleaded, 'Mr. Mack, don't take me out. Please. As hard as this hurts, it doesn't compare with what I've been through. Let me finish what I've started.'

" 'OK, go ahead, Lou,' the old skipper said. Painfully Lou picked himself up and went on to win nineteen games for Philadelphia that year."

Killibrew concluded his story with the comment: "Lou Brissi epitomizes what it takes to be successful in sports or business or life. I've never known a truly successful person who wasn't knocked off his feet a time or two. The one who excels is the one who, no matter how many times he's knocked down, always manages to get back up one more time."

Ann Kiemel Anderson, well-known writer, speaker, and author of eight books, one of which is *I'm Running to Win*, shared with me that preparing to run her first marathon was one of the hardest things she has ever done: "Dave, it taught me that to be faithful to a sport or athletic event, to be faithful to God, to physical health, or to anything, there's a price that has to be paid. And it is true—there is no gain without pain."

While having breakfast with Stan Smith, the former Wimbledon Tennis champ at Hilton Head Island, South Carolina, I asked him what the most difficult part was about playing the professional circuit.

"It's really hard to get yourself mentally up for every match," he explained. "Especially when you switch time zones and have spent all night on the airplane, traveling to get to another country to play a new tournament."

Stan Smith is a true professional, and performs regardless of how he feels. One of the biggest differences between top producers and those who never reach their potential is that the top producers perform consistently regardless of feelings.

Professionals stick to commitments. It may cost a little, but if an individual will form the habit of sticking to commitments, it will pay long-term dividends.

Coach John Wooden is someone who believes in keeping his commitments. This came out very clear-

Principle 4: Be a Professional

ly as he was sharing with me how he happened to come to UCLA as head basketball coach.

"My second year as head coach at Indiana State we were the runners-up for the National Championship at Kansas City. Offers from some larger universities started coming in. UCLA put in a bid. But since I played college ball for Purdue, I wanted to stay in the Big Ten. I had pretty well decided to take the position at the University of Minnesota. The athletic director was to obtain final approval from the board, and he was to call me at a specific time. The call didn't come. UCLA phoned, again offering me the head coaching position, and I accepted it. An hour later the call came from Minnesota."

"So, Coach, is it safe to assume that if the University of Minnesota had called you one hour earlier, you would have gone there instead?"

"That's correct. And if it hadn't been for a late April snowstorm that prevented the athletic director from getting to a phone, the call would have come on time. But since I had already given my word to UCLA, I didn't want to break it."

This gave me a tremendous insight into the character of the man who, while head coach at UCLA, won an unprecedented ten NCAA championships.

Another characteristic of a real pro is that he is teachable.

In talking to Coach Bill Hodges about Larry Byrd, I learned that Larry had developed a highly professional attitude long before turning pro. His being made NBA Rookie of the Year in '79-'80 demonstrated this very clearly.

"Larry never questioned anything I told him to

do," Coach Bill Hodges told me. "Larry's greatest characteristic is not necessarily his physical ability. It's his ability to make all his teammates relish playing with him. He's so unselfish. He's very humble and always willing to give the whole team credit for success. To him, success is something to be shared with his teammates.

"He has a phenomenal court awareness. He knows what's going to happen five seconds ahead—a blink of an eye before it happens. He has great concentration.

"Larry is not as good a shooter now as he was in college. He injured his finger. He messed it up bad, and he can't control the ball as well with that hand as he used to. But he has learned to compensate for that. He's always trying to improve. He never gets to the point where he thinks he knows it all."

Professionals realize that success is not a matter of chance, but of choices. A professional chooses to do whatever is necessary to reach his goal, whether he feels like it or not. He is willing to put forth that extra effort that the amateur considers too much trouble, too time consuming, or beneath his dignity. The pro is always learning, improving his skills, refining his expertise.

While attending a National Speakers Association meeting in New Orleans, I walked into a session on "How to Structure a Speech." Glancing around the room, I noticed an empty chair next to a friend of mine and his wife. I walked over, we exchanged smiles, and I sat down. While listening to the lecture, I wrote out a few of the speaker's ideas. Then I realized the man sitting beside me was taking many more notes than I was. I found this very interesting, be-

Principle 4: Be a Professional

cause not only was my friend a professional speaker himself, but I happened to know he earned about three times as much per speech as the man leading the session.

That really impressed me. Here was this craftsman concentrating so intently, trying to pick up a few new pointers, working continually to polish his already polished performance. I had to conclude that his attitude must be part of the reason he has over eight million books in print and continues to be in such high demand as a speaker. The friend I'm referring to is none other than that master storyteller himself, Og Mandino.

That kind of teachableness is another quality that marks a real professional. Back in the summer of 1970 I began to develop a few professional characteristics. It's a good thing too, because after that great day when I sold the 700 dollars' worth of books that enabled me to join my friends in the President's Club, I was in for a real letdown.

PRINCIPLE 5

Live in the Present

Coming off that $700 day, I was really flying high. The next Monday I had another good day and the same thing Tuesday. By Thursday morning I was sitting on $1,000 on schedule for another great week. I was feeling good, even though by 11:00 A.M. the day was already a scorcher, and I had had somewhat of a slow start.

Did I say *slow?* That's an understatement. I hadn't sold anything, but I was certain I was going to. Whenever I felt myself beginning to get discouraged, I'd read a couple of the little signs I'd taped to the metal dashboard of my faded green '53 Chevy. "Smile!" "Relax!" "Be enthusiastic!" they would remind me, and I'd stride confidently up to the next door. No sale.

OK, Dave, don't let it get to you, I'd tell myself. *You're picking up good names and building a good prospect list for this evening. It isn't really all that hot—just a normal warm summer day. Quit trying to figure out how you can last until 9:30 tonight. Just make it till noon.*

Now Is Your Time to Win

See that house? I'd ask myself.
Yeah.
Can you knock on that door?
Yeah.
Well, go knock on it then.
I'd give my sales pitch, but no sale. Then I'd tell myself, *See, I didn't sell there either.*
Wait a minute, we're not going to talk about that. That last house is history. See that next house?
Yeah.
Can you knock on that door?
Well, yeah, I guess I can knock on one more door.
Well, go do it. We'll talk about it later.
No sale.
See that next house? . . .

I'd keep playing these games with myself, trying to keep myself going, repeating positive slogans to keep me motivated. The hotter it got, the more tired I got of saying, "This is the best day I've ever had. I can, I will, I'm going to. . . ." But I did it anyway because I knew it would help me keep a positive attitude.

As I drove to the house, I checked out the dashboard again and noticed the picture of Babe Ruth smiling at me. The line under his picture was a reminder to me: "He just kept swinging." The Babe had been a pro, and when he'd get into a slump, he'd refuse to change his position at the plate, the way he held his bat, or his magnificent swing. He knew he was good, and that if he'd just be patient and keep swinging, he would start connecting. I was going to connect too! Confidently I tucked my shirttail into my slacks and marched up to the next house. No sale.

Determinedly I reminded myself, *That house is history. Forget it and go on to the next.* I climbed back into

Principle 5: Live in the Present

the Chevy and looked around for another encouraging word: "Remember Herman Osgood." That one always made me smile, because of course, no one remembered Herman Osgood—he quit. Well, I wasn't going to be a quitter! I approached the next front door, smiling optimistically.

No sale. My footsteps were dragging a bit as I returned to the car. This was getting a bit much. I wasn't even getting to make many demonstrations. And I was running out of signs on my dashboard. I sure wasn't ever going to pay off all my debts at this rate. With no job lined up for the future and all my time devoted to door-to-door selling, I had to make good this summer. *Whoa, wait a minute, David,* I commanded. *You're letting yourself slide down into self-pity, which does not help one bit!* The hardest thing to do is to live in the present. It's unrealistic to live in the future, and it's impossible to live in the past. The farthest thing away is a second ago. *So settle down and concentrate on the task before you. Now is all you have, so make the most of it.*

I knew logically that made a lot of sense, but all that good advice was hard to follow with the sun beating down on me and my scorecard reading zero. I stopped at a little country store and bought a Pepsi. Sipping it slowly, I thought, *Living in the present and concentrating on the task at hand seems obvious, but it's very hard to keep from thinking negative thoughts and worrying about the future when things aren't going well.*

It's impossible to think a negative thought and a positive thought at the same time, my mind shot back at me.

That's true, I admitted. *If I can just make myself think positive thoughts, then it becomes impossible for the negative ones to grab hold. I'll control my thinking.* Controlling my thoughts is the ultimate discipline. *And I'll do it!*

In that *thirty-second* conversation with myself, I had solidified another winning principle. Living in the present was the only logical way to tackle a difficult problem. I had learned from my past mistakes, and there was nothing else to be gained from rehearsing them. I could contemplate long-range goals during my leisure hours. The present was all I could control. Whether I felt like it or not, my present task was to knock on another door. So I finished my Pepsi and headed for another door.

A pleasant-faced lady answered and let me know she wasn't interested in buying anything from a door-to-door salesman. Her determination seemed to match my own. As I was continuing my conversation, she proceeded to close the door. I'd had only a few doors slammed in my face during my career, but a number of people had closed doors slowly while I was still talking.

As I was walking down the steps, I thought, *She really did seem very nice. I'll bet she has a good sense of humor.* On impulsive I dashed around the house to the back door and knocked. When she opened the door, she seemed a bit shocked to find me standing there smiling.

"What in the world do you want?" she gasped.

"Ma'am, I hope you are a whole lot friendlier than the lady I met at the front door," I replied with a smile.

I think she wanted to get mad, but she was so startled she actually started laughing. "Well, at least that's different," she admitted and then said, "Oh, come on in." I gave her an enthusiastic demonstration, and she bought a couple of books.

Principle 5: Live in the Present

That sale, I felt certain, had turned my day around. Now there would be no stopping me. But it didn't work. To my great chagrin it seemed as if I could not give a book away. When I pulled into the restaurant that night, I had a grand total of $40 in sales. My commission was about $16, a slight comedown from my $700 day when I'd cleared close to $300, but I was determined not to let it get me discouraged. *Today is over, Dave. Just chalk it up to experience,* I told myself. So I did.

The next morning I rolled out of bed and repeated a prayer by Hartsill Wilson that Mort Utley had shared with us in sales school:

> This is the beginning of a new day. God has given me this day to use as I will. I can waste it or use it for good. What I do today is important because I'm exchanging a day of my life for it. When tomorrow comes, this day will be gone forever, leaving in its place something that I have traded for it. I want it to be gain, not loss; good, not evil; success, not failure. In order that I shall not regret the price I paid for it, may I have sufficient wisdom and courage that this shall be my record for today.

After breakfast I returned to the same sales locality and sold over $400. The days all averaged out, and I ended up with about $1,800 for the week. It came about because I'd stuck to the principle I'd been learning, the one about living in the present.

Each day I tried to concentrate on making that day a success. I'd tell myself, *If you can have a successful day,*

Now Is Your Time to Win

you can have a successful week, summer, year, career. I don't know if I can work this hard the rest of my life, but I can work hard today. Now is my time to win.

Marijohn Wilkin wrote the famous song that expresses this same sentiment. "One Day at a Time" is probably the best known of the one hundred-plus songs this member of the Nashville Songwriters' Hall of Fame has written. When I interviewed her in her lovely suburban home, I asked her what had inspired her to write the song by which so many people identified her.

"It wasn't inspiration as much as a total need for help," she replied in her usual frank manner. "It was about eight years ago, and it had been a bad year. My mother had just died. My marriage was on the rocks. My business partner had left me, and I had never been into publishing alone before. It seemed like the old domino theory—just one thing after another.

"So I just sat down at the piano, and I sang that whole chorus—just as if it were written on the piano. I just sang it, and I knew it was a great song. I wrote it down as fast as I could. Then I jumped up and called Kris Kristofferson, who had worked for me before he went off and got so famous. 'Man, I've written a hit!' I told him.

"The chorus I just sang out, and the second verse came really easy, but being a professional writer who works at my craft, I knew the verse I had was not the way the song was supposed to start. Kris came over and helped me put together the first verse."

"Has the philosophy of the song helped you in your own life?" I asked.

"Oh, yes! I still try to live that way," she stated. "There's just so much you can do in a day, and you

Principle 5: Live in the Present

are in trouble if you start worrying about what's coming. You *cannot* live in the past. If you have had a bad hurt in your life, that's sad, but that goes with living. I feel sorry for people who constantly live either in the past or on a promise of the future. What's the matter with right now? Right now is the time to live to its fullest."

The words of her song "One Day at a Time" express her philosophy beautifully:

One day at a time, sweet Jesus,
That's all I'm asking from you.
Just give me the strength to do every day
What I have to do.
Yesterday's gone, sweet Jesus,
And tomorrow may never be mine.
Lord, help me today, show me the way
One day at a time.

When a successful man who knows his business and is professional in all he does has reversals because of circumstances he cannot control, that's the time to live in the present. J. Fred Landers, former executive vice-president and now full-time consultant to The Southwestern Company, had this experience. He started out in the book business as a student in 1935. He was doing fine in building a strong sales organization until he was called into the service in World War II.

"When I got out," he said, "the student managers I had worked with before the service were scattered everywhere, and I had only 4 left. They recruited 16 students between them, and I recruited 15 for my personal team. That gave us a total of 31 salespeople.

The next year I had 75. In '48 I built up to 155. Then in '49 I had 313 salespeople."

Those were 100 percent increases three years in a row. Not only was that impressive, but it was the only time in the history of The Southwestern Company that a sales manager had ever done it.

"But then the Korean War came on in 1950, and I dropped to 175," he continued. "A lot of my student managers were going into the service. It was hard to recruit new students because they were being drafted right and left.

"The key to growth is the student managers, and I didn't have a lot of control over getting them back. I found it's a lot harder to build an organization than to maintain it. It took me until 1954 to grow back to 300.

"But I had a system I knew worked, and I kept on working it. I knew from experience I could rebuild. I had grown to over four hundred salespeople when the Vietnam War started, and I was faced with the same problem all over again."

"How did you learn to live in the present in situations you couldn't control?" I asked him.

"Well, first I was committed to the business. I never gave serious thought to giving up. I was determined to stay and build a great sales organization. I knew this was what I wanted to do. The minute someone in a profession starts vacillating between staying or leaving, he doesn't put as much effort into it. I knew I'd just have to rebuild all over again.

"I went on to become part-owner, and we built the company from a sales force of 800 to over 4,600 in less than ten years."

I've known Fred Landers for many years now, and

Principle 5: Live in the Present

I know he never allows situations he can't control to keep him from living in the present. He has formed the habit of concentrating on the task he has before him, and this has enabled him to succeed in spite of difficulties that would have made a weaker man give up.

I was talking to Coach Bear Bryant a few days after Alabama beat Penn State, enabling him to tie Alonzo Stagg's 314-game win record. I asked him, "What's going through your mind being just one game short of becoming the winningest coach in the history of football?"

"The only thing I'm thinking about is how to beat Auburn University—and in an intellectual way at that. And all this other whoopla stuff going on around us I try not to think about too much."

This is a man who knows how to live in the present. Instead of basking in the glory of past accomplishments or of the honors certain to come his way in the future, he concentrates on the major task at hand. Mental discipline has had a lot to do with the phenomenal success that Coach Bear Bryant has had. The following week, history was made when Alabama beat Auburn.

Tom Landry, coach of the Dallas Cowboys, also mentioned something about concentration when I interviewed him. "Concentration," he assured me, "is one of the most important habits anyone can develop. Once you allow other things to come into your mind and break your concentration, you can't function the same.

"Some people say I'm not emotional. What I'm doing is concentrating on what's happening," he explained. "I can't cheer the great play that just happened. I have to be thinking about what the opposition may do next. If I show emotion, I break my concentration. I keep my eyes on the game. If I even look at the scoreboard, I've broken my concentration."

Athletes can teach us all a lot about living in the present. Bill Wade, who quarterbacked the Chicago Bears to a national championship, is now a banker in Nashville and is a good friend of mine. While traveling with him to a speaking engagement, I asked him, "What's the greatest challenge in professional football?"

After a little hesitation, he replied, "Concentration." He shared an experience that took place on an extremely hot day in training camp in Rennselaer, Indiana. "The sun was beating down and I wasn't looking forward to eight hours of practice. My mind was on myself, Dave. When your mind is on yourself, nothing tends to go quite as well as it should. We had a big game coming up in just two weeks. I was feeling a lot of pressure. How was I going to do in the first game? Would my arm be in good shape?

"I was also thinking of the people who were watching us practice, the coaches, the other players. A lot of attention was on me as the quarterback. All these things were bothering me. Finally, I just told myself, *'Hey, I've got to block this stuff out. I've got to get my mind off myself and concentrate on what I'm doing right now.'*

"So I did. I took the ball, cocked my arm, and fired right into the chest area of the receiver who was warming up with me. He threw the ball back and again I faded back and fired, heading in a second time right on target. I just kept throwing the ball back and concentrating on hitting the target.

Principle 5: Live in the Present

"Then an interesting thing happened. As I was concentrating totally on what I was doing, I forgot the heat. I forgot about the eight hours of practice. I forgot about the people watching. I even forgot about the big game coming up. I really began enjoying just throwing the ball."

A winning principle in football, selling, or anything else in life is living in the present and concentrating on the immediate challenge. When you're living in the present, your mind is zeroing in on what you have to do right now. One of the greatest advocates of this principle is motivational speaker Charlie "Tremendous" Jones, author of the best seller *Life Is Tremendous.*

"You live in the present because the future takes care of itself. The past is done. You live in the present when you learn there is nothing else but the present," Charlie declared. "That doesn't mean you don't plan. It means you don't spend *all* your time dreaming. Dreaming is great—if you're doing it in bed! But *now* is the time to *work!*

"What keeps many people from living in the present? Getting so bogged down from what they did yesterday—and so scared to death about what is going to happen tomorrow—that they just can't get anything done today. It cripples them. I'm an authority on the subject because I am the worst offender. But at least I'm ahead of most people, because I realize I'm an offender. And once you realize what you're doing wrong, you can do something about it.

"If I find myself getting concerned about tomorrow or feeling bad about yesterday, my subconscious says, *'Pal, you'd better get to doing what you gotta do, or you are just compounding your problem.*' That's what self-motivation is all about—training your subconscious. You develop this the same way you develop any habit. You start with the simplest habit, and then you build the next one. You don't worry about the big ones until you settle the simple ones. After learning that, you can capitalize on what you've got to do—whether you like it or not. That's what determines your future."

Charlie is conscious of the importance of living in the present. He has developed the habit of controlling his thoughts by keeping his mind centered on a definite plan of action. By doing this, he can eliminate negative thoughts that could keep him from performing at top capacity. Living in the present allows him to have a positive attitude which can make a great difference in the ultimate results in any situation.

An optimistic outlook on life is a great asset, and can help you live in the present. Mort Utley's story about the young optimist is the best I've heard on the subject. He has told it for thirty-six years, sharing it yearly in sales school. It goes like this:

There were parents who had six-year-old twin boys, who were extreme opposites. One of them was the world's greatest optimist; he loved everybody and everything. The other one was the world's best pessimist; he hated everybody and everything. The parents were so disturbed by the extreme opposite characteristics in these two boys that they took them to a psychiatrist. They said, "You've got to help us. We just don't know what to do."

The psychiatrist declared, "I can't imagine two boys in the same family, especially twins, being such

Principle 5: Live in the Present

extreme opposites. But I have a test for boys like this."

So, the parents and the doctor took the little extreme pessimist down to a room that had every kind of toy a child could imagine. The psychiatrist said, "Sonny, all of these are yours. You have a good time, and we'll come back after a while." They went out and shut the door.

Then they took the little extreme optimist down to a room that didn't have one thing in it except a great big pile of horse manure right in the middle of the floor. The psychiatrist said, "Sonny, have a good time, and we'll come back after a while."

In about twenty minutes the parents and the doctor went to the room where the little pessimist was. He was seated in the middle of the floor with his arms folded. He hadn't touched a single toy.

The psychiatrist asked, "Sonny, why didn't you ride on that rocking horse?"

"I was afraid I'd fall off and break my arm."

"Well, why didn't you skate on the roller skates? That would have been fun."

"I was afraid I'd fall down and skin my knees."

"Well, why didn't you blow up those balloons? Those balloons get real big, and they've got pictures on them."

"I was afraid I'd hurt my mouth."

"Why didn't you eat some of that candy? That's good candy. All the kids like that candy."

"I was afraid I'd get a stomachache."

The psychiatrist turned to the parents and admitted, "He's in pretty bad shape. But let's go see what the other boy is doing."

They returned to the second room. When they

opened the door, the kid was bent down over the horse manure, slinging it just as hard as he could. He had it all over the ceiling, all over the walls, all over the floor, all over himself.

The psychiatrist took one look and said, "Sonny, what in the world are you doing?"

The little boy looked up at him and grinned. "With all this manure, there's got to be a pony in here somewhere!"

In sales school, after the laughter dies down, Mort continues: "I'm going to let you in on a little secret. Don't tell anybody. But this summer you're going to have to wade through an awful lot of it. But just remember, the more there is, the bigger the ponies."

While working on this chapter, I decided to include one rather lengthy quote because it has meant so much to me, and has been a great help in keeping me focused on the present. I had no idea who had written the short essay titled "Just For Today," but I knew it was widely distributed by Alcoholics Anonymous, so I put in a call to their offices in New York City.

A gentleman named Robert P. told me: "Taking it one day at a time is so central to the recovery program in AA that the principle has been passed on from one sponsor to another since the founding of the organization. Strangely enough, I don't recall anything in our basic literature about living a day at a time. It has always been one of the most important parts of the AA program of recovery."

"What if I were an alcoholic?" I asked him. "How would you help me get through one day?"

"I would tell you exactly that. I'd say, 'Do you think

Principle 5: Live in the Present

you could stay away from a drink for one day?' And you might say, 'I don't know.'

" 'What about an hour? All right. If that's too long, what about five minutes? Good, well, then in five minutes, we will talk about it again.' "

"So you would actually walk people through a day?" I asked.

"Yes, we do it all the time. In my own case I encountered this idea after my first AA meeting. Incidentally, my sponsor was a citizen in high standing, drove a Porsche, had a black belt in karate, and had an obvious zest for life. He had had about thirteen years of sobriety.

"At the end of the meeting, he asked what I thought of it, and I said, 'Not much. How can you be so cheerful when you know you're never going to have another drink the rest of your life?'

"He said, 'Oh, I haven't quit drinking for the rest of my life.' Of course, my ears perked up immediately at that.

" 'Oh, no?' I responded.

" 'No. I could drink tomorrow,' he said. 'In fact, considering my life history, some people would think it quite likely that I might drink tomorrow, but I haven't had a drink today. It's 9:00 P.M. and I believe I can make it to midnight. When tomorrow morning comes, I'll get down on my knees and ask God to help me stay away from a drink for that day, too.'

"Then it began to dawn on me that this was the way you did it. You don't have to quit for the rest of your life. Only quit for today. It's incredible! All I did was quit for today, and before I knew it, I had twenty-five years of sobriety."

Robert informed me that AA didn't have a copyright on the essay I wanted to use, and assured me it would be fine to reprint it. Then after I hung up, I got to thinking about what he had said, and the more I thought about it, the clearer it seemed that this principle could be applied to most of the problems people face. It sounds so simple, yet most people don't live in the present. Many will never reach their potential because they waste so much time reliving the past or worrying about the future. Reading the following each morning can help develop the habit of living in the present:

JUST FOR TODAY

JUST FOR TODAY I will try to live through this day only, and not tackle my whole life problem at once. I can do something for twelve hours that would appall me if I felt that I had to keep it up for a lifetime.

JUST FOR TODAY I will be happy. This assumes to be true what Abraham Lincoln said, "Most folks are as happy as they make up their minds to be."

JUST FOR TODAY I will adjust myself to what is, and not try to adjust everything to my own desires. I will take my "luck" as it comes, and fit myself to it.

JUST FOR TODAY I will try to strengthen my mind. I will study. I will learn something useful. I will not be a mental loafer. I will read something that requires effort, thought, and concentration.

JUST FOR TODAY I will exercise my soul in three ways: I will do somebody a good turn,

Principle 5: Live in the Present

and not get found out; if anybody knows of it, it will not count. I will do at least two things I don't want to do—just for exercise. I will not show anyone that my feelings are hurt; they may be hurt, but today I will not show it.

JUST FOR TODAY I will be agreeable. I will look as well as I can, dress becomingly, talk low, act courteously, criticize not one bit, not find fault with anything, and not try to improve or regulate anybody except myself.

JUST FOR TODAY I will have a program. I may not follow it exactly, but I will have it. I will save myself from two pests: hurry and indecision.

JUST FOR TODAY I will have a quiet half hour all by myself, and relax. During this half hour, sometime, I will try to get a better perspective on my life.

JUST FOR TODAY I will be unafraid. Especially I will not be afraid to enjoy what is beautiful, and to believe that as I give to the world, so the world will give to me.

PRINCIPLE 6

Do Your Best

The long, hot summer days quickly turned into weeks, and I found myself in the home stretch and running well. Then I opened the envelope containing The Southwestern Company's top-contender list —the total ranking of the top salespeople to date. I was elated to discover I was number six on the list.

News like that just had to be shared, so I put in a call to California. "I've got great news, dad!" I exploded. "I just found out I rank number six out of the 700 salespeople I'm in competition with in my division."

"That's great news. We're really proud of the progress you're making this summer."

"Now I'm faced with a new challenge."

"What's that, Dave?"

"I just realized there is a possibility I could be number one. But what if I really pull out all the stops and go for it and then don't make it?"

"If you don't do your best, you won't make it. But, if you do your best and still don't make it, you're still a winner."

Now Is Your Time to Win

"Huh?"

"What if you really do your best and you don't end up at the top? There is nothing more important than knowing you have done your best. Doing your best is more important than being number one. It's more important than selling more books than 699 others. When you know you have done your best, you win self-respect.

"You've done well this summer, Dave, and your mother and I couldn't be more proud of you. It sounds to me as if you really want to aim for that number-one spot, so "Go for it!' Give it all you've got. Just remember you can't control what your competitors are doing. You can control yourself and your own performance. Just give it your best shot!"

"It's really kinda amazing to think I'm even in contention, but you're right. All I can do is my best. Win or lose, I'm going to try. I'm going to do everything I can to be number one, but if I don't make it, it won't be because I didn't try."

"Dave, just remember, we love you, and we'll be pulling for you."

"Thanks, dad. That means a lot."

After I'd hung up, I thought about just how much it did mean to know my folks had confidence in me. Having a dependable source of encouragement is an invaluable asset.

My father was also one of the best examples I'd ever seen of a man who continually did his best, regardless of the circumstances. As the head of the music department at different universities, he had always been a builder. He'd also taken on the responsibility as choir director at a number of churches and, often starting from scratch, would consistently pro-

Principle 6: Do Your Best

duce fantastic choirs. He's a real professional and seems to have a gift for building and bringing out the best in people, which is one of the reasons he has become one of the best music directors in the country.

Thinking about my folks made me realize there is more to having a rich life than just accumulating a lot of money. My parents have a life rich in friends, in music, in accomplishment, and in the knowledge that they have inspired many others along the way. They have taught me that real success is not measured in just dollars and cents. *Real success is the personal satisfaction that comes from knowing that you have done your best to reach your fullest potential in what you have chosen to do.*

With this attitude I began my campaign for the coveted spot at the top. I was feeling good about my chances of making it when a call came from George Butler in Nashville: "Dave, we are in the process of hiring a district sales manager for next year, and I've been sharing with Spencer Hays how well you've been doing this summer. He wants you to take the next flight to Nashville to talk about coming with The Southwestern Company on a professional basis."

For once in my life I was speechless. I had looked at the sales managers in The Southwestern Company as men on white horses! To me, they were the epitome of success in business. They had not only a good financial opportunity, but also the opportunity to influence young people in a very positive way.

"Dave, are you still there?"

"Huh, oh, yeah, George, I'm here. What should I wear? And what about the rest of the summer?"

"Spencer won't care what you wear," he laughed. "And you'll still have time to get back on the book field and finish out the summer. I'll look forward to seeing you at the airport."

On the flight to Nashville, I contemplated meeting Spencer Hays. *The* Spencer Hays. He held several records with The Southwestern Company, and in my mind was a real pro. The more I thought about actually talking with him, the more nervous I became. Not even the new grey pin-striped suit I had just bought for the occasion could overcome the feeling of inadequacy that was welling up inside me.

Now, wait a minute, Dave, I reprimanded myself. *You're not maintaining a professional attitude. You keep up this negative thinking and you're going to blow the interview. Aren't you always saying that the best sales talk in the world is the truth? OK, so now you're going to try to sell yourself. Just apply the same principle. Be yourself. Relax. Do your best.*

George Butler and his wife, Harriet, met me at the airport and whisked me off to the plush St. Clair's Restaurant where we were greeted by the very distinguished Spencer Hays. His dark eyes sparkled under his thick eyebrows, and the rest of his face was lighted by a big smile. "Hi, there! My name is Spencer Hays," he said while extending his hand. "I've heard so many good things about you that it is an honor and a privilege to be standing in the presence of one of the greatest salesmen in the company."

I was a little embarrassed by the flattery, but enjoyed it just the same. We ordered our meals and proceeded to have a very pleasant conversation. Spencer asked me a bit about my background, but very little reference was made to my being a sales manager. After about an hour of casual conversation,

Principle 6: Do Your Best

he paused, looked me in the eye, and asked, "Dave, can you recruit?"

I swallowed hard, and hesitated for what seemed like about *thirty seconds* while I reviewed the seven principles I had developed during the summer. They had helped me have a successful summer, and the firm conviction developed in me that those same principles could help me become a successful sales manager.

"Yes, sir," I replied with newly found confidence. "I can."

Spencer looked at me thoughtfully for a moment and then with no comment in response to my reply, said, "Meet me in my office tomorrow at 10:00 A.M., and we'll talk more about it."

The next morning, after a very extensive interview, I flew back to the book field with instructions to call Spencer in three days. During that waiting period I found it harder than ever to concentrate on the task at hand. My mind kept gravitating to the question, "Do I or don't I have the much-desired position?"

Wednesday about noon I placed the call. "Spencer, this is Dave Dean."

"Hi, Dave! I've been expecting you to call. A lot of thought has been given to this decision, and I'm happy to inform you that I am looking forward to working with you in the capacity of a district sales manager. We're proud to have you with The Southwestern Company."

When I hung up the phone, I let out a sigh of utter contentment. I had the job. Dad was right—doing my best did pay. I still didn't know if I was going to be number one in my division, but I was already a winner. I'd won a coveted position with one of the top direct-sales firms in the nation.

Tracy Caulkins has been swimming her best since she started competing at age eleven. Now, at age nineteen, she holds fifteen American records, and is the only swimmer to have ever won five gold medals at the world championships.

I was talking with Tracy a few days after she'd broken Johnny Weissmuller's fifty-year-old record—becoming winner of more national championships than any swimmer in American history.

"How much time do you spend in the water?" I asked her.

"I train four-and-a-half to five hours a day, six days a week. I've been doing that for the last five years."

"How do you keep yourself motivated to work that hard, Tracy?"

"Well, you look at the goals you have for yourself and for your team, and you know you aren't going to reach those goals unless you train hard. Working toward a goal makes you keep at it. All along I've just tried to do the best I could, and all these titles have just sort of happened."

"So you consider all your success a result of the habit of doing your best?"

"Right. To do my best I've got to work as hard as I can at practices. Then when I swim a race or compete, I concentrate on doing my best. The workouts give me confidence that I will be able to do my best. My main priority is to win, but if I get second or third place and I know I did the best I could, that's OK. If

Principle 6: Do Your Best

I lose and I know I could have done something better, that's frustrating."

"What did you feel like when you were about to swim the race that would break Weissmuller's record?"

"I wasn't thinking about the all-time record, actually. I was just trying to concentrate on that one race, trying to win and do the best I could. After I'd won it, I felt, well, you know, honored. I guess it's quite an accomplishment, but I really don't think it's going to hit me for a while. Right now I'm just looking toward the world championships in Ecuador this summer. My main goal for this season is to do well there."

"Do you have any advice for young swimmers?" was my final question.

"Well, just to continue to train and have fun. And don't worry if you don't seem to be improving, because it will come if you keep concentrating and working hard. Success will come if you continue to do your best."

The importance of doing your best was illustrated by another great swimmer, John Naber. He told me that his goal in the 100-meter backstroke in the 1976 Olympics had not been to win a medal, but to swim the distance in 55.5 seconds. "I told myself if I went 55.5 and someone else went 55.3, there would be no reason for disappointment," John shared with me. "I'd still be a success. I would hit my goal on the money and I'd have done my best."

The record book shows that he won the 100-meter backstroke in 55.49. He beat his goal by a one-hundredth of a second. Winning the gold medal was a nice bonus. If someone else had won it, John wouldn't have been bitter. Either way he would have won.

One of the most difficult things to face is the possibility of doing your best and working as hard as you can while your efforts seem to go unrewarded. This is especially true if you have gotten off schedule and are finding it difficult to get back to doing whatever is necessary to succeed. Then it is time to return to principle number one—accept your situation exactly as it is—and start working all seven principles over again.

Jim Calder found himself in this situation shortly after he became a district sales manager with The Southwestern Company in 1970. Sales managers are rated primarily on their ability to increase business, and Jim's first year he worked harder than he ever had in his life to do just that. Yet he only increased 6.8 percent. His second year he redoubled his efforts and saw a 16 percent increase. Other sales managers were seeing increases of 40, 60, and 100 percent in a single year. Jim hung in there and kept plugging away, yet in his third year his business increased only 4.4 percent.

Then in 1974 all his persistence and dedication paid off. He grew 86 percent, earning more in that year than he had in his first three years together. The next two years he set several recruiting and production records that still stand. I asked him how he managed to keep doing his best during those discouraging years when he wasn't producing well.

"I had a few good cries," he confided. "I was broken up inside because I didn't reach my goals. I did a lot of rationalizing. I got mad at my boss because I felt he had talked me into a job that was ridiculously difficult, if not impossible. Then I got mad at myself,

Principle 6: Do Your Best

because others were succeeding where I was failing. Finally I came to understand one fundamental truth. The problem was me. Because, if there was one other man in the company who was highly successful, then it was possible to do it. The responsibility, therefore, was not with management or the company or the territory, but with *me*.

"With that in mind I asked myself, *Do you really want to accomplish something with your life? If you really, really do, then you are not in a battle with the business. You are in a battle over whether you will ever be anything or not.* I had a choice of going off into other businesses, but I felt that the results would probably be the same until I, Jim Calder, became the kind of individual who could rise to the occasion under any circumstances. I decided I couldn't win by quitting.

"I'm convinced that all of us have to win this battle with self if we really want to accomplish something with our lives. The battlefield might not be the book field; it can be an athletic arena or some other discipline, but you've got to win this war with self. Only then can you truly do your best in whatever you attempt."

Coach John Wooden also had some interesting things to say about doing your best. "No player of mine at UCLA ever heard me mention winning. I was constantly talking to them about doing the best they were capable of doing, to try to make the most of their own potential. I'd remind them that they could have no bearing on what others can do, but they could have control of themselves.

"I believe that if you do your best, the scores will be more to your liking. Before every game I would say, 'When the game is over, let's be able to hold our heads high—and the score will have nothing to do with that.'

"My definition of success is the self-satisfaction of knowing you have done the best you are capable of doing."

It's evident that Coach Wooden has applied that same philosophy to his private life, for he has twice been selected California's "Father of the Year."

Not all winners become household names. For years my travels through the Atlanta Airport were brightened by conversations with David T. Wyatt, who had the valet service in the men's room. David always had a great attitude, was cheerful, and took pride in his work. Although he had a limited education, he accepted his situation and worked hard to accomplish his goal of putting his three daughters through college.

"I worked twelve hours a day, seven days a week," David, who is now semiretired, told me. "I had my bad moments, but most people appreciated me. Lots of them would compliment me, and I got to know many of them.

"My daughters? Oh, they are all fine," he announced with evident pride. "One is a high school teacher, another teaches in elementary school, and the third is in civil service."

In my eyes, David T. Wyatt is a successful man. He's done his best with what he has and has maintained a great attitude while doing it.

Chris Bonds is another real winner and a young man I'm proud to call my friend. His senior year in high school at Brentwood Academy in Nashville, he received the Founders' Award given to the student

Principle 6: Do Your Best

who best exemplified excellence in sports, Christian leadership, and academic achievement. He also received the physics and the history awards for being number one in those subjects. All of this in spite of the fact that Chris is afflicted with Duchenne muscular dystrophy, the most severe of some forty types of muscular dystrophies.

"When I was five, my parents noticed I was falling down a lot," Chris recalled. "I got weaker and weaker until at age eight I was using a wheel chair full-time. My parents had to put me through exercises to keep my muscles from going. It hurt so much that I would cry out, but if they hadn't done it, I would have deteriorated a lot faster.

"In junior high I went through a period of feeling worthless. I wasn't really bitter, just disappointed and depressed sometimes. Then in high school it was tough to watch the others dating and all. Later I realized I had something to give and that the Lord had put me in this situation for a reason. I chose to do the best I could in my circumstances."

And Chris has done his best. After graduation from high school he received a good offer from Truckstops Corporation of America. Chris works as a computer programmer, and is one of the few in the country who are afflicted with Duchenne muscular dystrophy, and still hold a full-time job.

Nashville's WTVF-TV did a film entitled *The Winner*. It was an inspiring thirty-minute story about Chris and how he has been able to keep on keeping on during his fight with *MD*. In 1980 the film won the national Sylvester "Pat" Weaver Award for outstanding broadcasting contribution in the war against muscular dystrophy and other neuro-muscular related diseases. Chris has been a tremendous inspiration to me as he has been to everyone who has known him.

Cheryl Prewitt Blackwood, the lovely young lady who after five years of trying finally became Miss America 1980, has also had to learn to overcome physical difficulties. "When I was eleven, I was in an accident," she confided to me. "My left leg was crushed, my back was cracked, and I had over 100 stitches in my face. I've never had any plastic surgery. I was sewn up in the emergency room, and this is how it came out.

"Some people in this world are very beautiful, Dave, but I'm not one of them. I work very hard to be in the best physical shape I can be in. I make the most of my hair, makeup, and clothes. That's important to me. I want to do my best in everything.

"Negative self-images usually come from comparing oneself to others. I cannot be someone else, so I just try to be the very best Cheryl I can be. By being the best I can be, eventually I will get somewhere."

Coach Ed Temple, women's track coach at Tennessee State in Nashville, is used to challenging young women to do their best. His "Tigerbelles" have captured thirty-one national championships, eleven Olympic gold medals, five silver medals, and four bronzes. When budget cuts wouldn't allow him to send a team to the 1981 national championships, he determined to raise the money somehow by himself.

"I was really peeved," he admitted, "because I had a good team. I got some different organizations to

Principle 6: Do Your Best

sponsor us, but I still had only enough money to take four girls. That meant I had to leave some of my best girls home, because I wanted to give my sophomores some experience.

"They got out there and did their best, but I wasn't really keeping up with the points, because I knew we didn't have a chance. I didn't realize until they announced it that we had actually won the national championship with just four girls. Our girls had fifteen points, and the nearest team had only twelve! It was one of the highlights of my coaching career."

Coach Temple coached Wilma Rudolph to the Olympics. "When Wilma went to the Olympics in Australia in 1956, her hometown folks all thought she should win first place. I didn't expect it of her. She was too young. It was a great honor and a good experience for her just to be in the Olympic games. We had six girls on that team, and she was about the fifth fastest. She came in third in the relay race. She had done her best. But she wasn't satisfied. She came home and improved on her best until in the 1960 Olympics she became the first woman in the history of track and field to win three gold medals—a record that still stands."

Ed Temple knows how to deal with winners, because he is one himself. He has produced more Olympic runners than any other coach, and is also the only track coach to be selected three times to coach the United States Olympic Team. When Ed was nominated for the fourth time, he turned down the honor. He told me, "I was the first name nominated, but I'd already had three opportunities. Besides, there were others who deserved the recognition."

Now Is Your Time to Win

One of the areas where many people fear they won't perform at their best is in standing before a large group of people and speaking. Since this is essential in so many occupations—whether it is presenting a new idea to the board of directors or reporting to the stockholders of a large corporation—I asked Don Thoren, the president of The National Speakers Association, for a few tips on how people could overcome this difficulty.

"I think the fear of public speaking is born out of concern for self," he replied. "The real solution to the problem is to put your concern and emphasis on the other person. If you see yourself as one who is trying to help another, you're not nearly as self-conscious. The greatest quality any communicator can have is a belief in what he is saying and a desire to help the listener. When you put those two things together, the focus is taken off yourself, and you learn to become a better communicator."

Don is also the founder and president of The Thoren Group, a professional training company in sales, management, and personnel programs. His extremely relaxed, poised presence on the platform gives credibility to his advice on how to do your best at presenting your thoughts to others.

It has been said that results command respect and that a person's record of performance is all the recommendation he will ever need. Consequently, when it was announced in 1980 that Jerry Heffel had become president of The Southwestern Company, no one was really surprised. Jerry Heffel is a brilliant businessman, an exceptionally well-organized executive, and a real master in the art of dealing with people. He rose to the top of the multi-million dollar

Principle 6: Do Your Best

direct-sales company through daily dedication to doing his best. When Jerry Heffel talks about doing your best, people listen.

When I interviewed Jerry for "The Winner's Circle," Jerry shared with the radio audience some of the following tips:

"If you'll always work hard and do more than you're asked or expected to do, then you'll always be succeeding.

"The hardest time to do your best is on a day-to-day basis, because it is not as exciting. That's when it really takes a tremendous amount of dedication and commitment to keep doing your best.

"We need to take what we do very seriously, but not take ourselves too seriously.

"The habit of reacting positively to negative circumstances is one of the most important criteria for doing your best consistently.

"Doing your best is a habit—a way of life."

Men like Jerry Heffel have made The Southwestern Company what it is today—a thriving book business dedicated to developing character in young people.

Having trained over 50,000 of these young people over the last twelve years, I've had the opportunity of meeting some of the outstanding college students in America today.

One who stands out in my mind is Melvin Lee Davis, a young man dedicated to doing his best in every area of his life. Melvin came from a black family of ten children in South Carolina. As one of seventeen blacks in a student body of about 2,500 at Furman University in South Carolina, he received the Most Outstanding Freshman Award. While working his way through college, he still had time to be a student leader and served as vice-president of the student body in his junior year and narrowly missed being elected president his senior year.

In 1972, Melvin's first summer in The Southwestern Company's program, he went selling in a small city in Texas. Not owning a car didn't discourage him a bit. He carried his sales case from house to house as he walked up and down the streets. His retail business was $4,913 his first summer. Not a company record, but a solid summer.

When setting goals for his second summer, he just said, "I'm going to do the best I can and try to increase 100 percent." He did his best and increased his retail sales to $10,963. His third summer his retail business was $14,961. His fourth, he retailed $26,709. And his fifth he retailed an impressive $33,398, making $14,361 in commissions and finishing number six out of 6,505 salespeople. Because Melvin Davis was committed to doing his best, in time he became one of the very best.

Through the years, Melvin and I became good friends. Because of his record with The Southwestern Company, he was invited to become a full-time sales manager, and he and his wife, Jackie, moved to Nashville shortly before the birth of their first child. With his good-natured, upbeat personality, Melvin made friends easily. His optimistic outlook on life made him fun to be with. He loved life so much that he made people enjoy it, too. That's why the phone call that told of his death in a traffic accident came as such a shock.

Jackie asked me to come to South Carolina for the funeral to deliver the eulogy. I was honored to be

Principle 6: Do Your Best

asked, yet I felt totally inadequate to put into words what a fine young man Melvin had been and how much he had meant to everyone who had known him. All I could promise was that I would do my best.

Sitting on the platform of the little black country church, I looked over the crowd that had gathered to honor Melvin's memory. The wood-framed building had a seating capacity of about 100, but nearly twice that many people had squeezed in. It was the most unusual combination of people I had ever seen. Scattered among the home folks were former classmates from Furman and book people from The Southwestern Company. His best friend, Ron Hooker; his student manager, Marvin Hall; his former sales manager, Terry Weaver; and President Jerry Heffel were all standing in the crowded aisles.

Then they wheeled in Jackie. Her left foot, which had been injured in the accident, was bound in a cast. On her lap she held her beautiful seventeen-month-old daughter, Charsie. A slender slip of a girl, Jackie displayed a remarkable amount of courage as they parked her wheelchair to the left of the casket. Her composure had to come from the One who is the Source of real peace. As Onnie Kirk, Melvin's director of sales, was finishing his remarks, I prayed, "Lord, help me to say something that will be meaningful for Jackie."

"My first reaction when I heard of the tragedy was to ask, 'Why?' " I began. "Why would God take someone like Melvin Davis? Such a capable young man. So dedicated. So in love with life and with so much to give.

"Sorrow is universal, and none of us can escape it. The world is full of pain, suffering, accidents, and despair. But 'the God of all comfort' can be our refuge. Jesus promised, 'In my Father's house are many mansions.... I go to prepare a place for you.' We have the assurance that Melvin has triumphed over death. He lives eternally.

"Yet we miss him. God never promised we would not suffer in this life, but he has promised to give us the courage to face our sorrows. We are all saddened by our loss, yet we can be thankful we had the privilege of knowing Melvin Davis. He enriched my life as he did all those who knew and loved him.

"When I think of Melvin, the word *commitment* comes to mind. He was a committed student. A committed sales manager. A committed Christian. A committed husband and father. Many people live long lives, yet can't count on one hand the people they have influenced for good. Melvin had but a short number of years, yet he influenced more lives than most people who have lived two or three times as long. And that influence will live on.

"Jackie, we know your loss is great. We loved him, too. Little Charsie doesn't understand what has happened and what she has lost. As she matures, she will discover that her dad was quite a man. He always did his best."

In the years since that touching experience, Melvin's memory has continued to be an inspiration to me. Not only because he always did his best, but also because he was a living example of the seventh principle. This, the most important of all the principles, is the foundation upon which all the others are built.

PRINCIPLE 7

Let God Help You

The sun was shining, and I was singing at full volume in my off-key tenor as I drove toward Nashville. My old green Chevy had given up the ghost, and I had invested in a classy-looking '52 Oldsmobile to pull my U-haul full of books back to headquarters. Life was sweet. I was number one! I'd made it to the top. I was about to begin my career as a district sales manager for The Southwestern Company.

Interstate 75 cut through a mountain pass, and there was Chattanooga laid out at my feet. The magnificent view seemed symbolic of the world stretched out before me. Even though my total commissions of $9,300 that summer wouldn't cover my $15,000 debt, it had put a good-sized dent in it. Oh, the thrill of victory.

As I whistled a romantic little ditty, my thoughts turned to Suzie Taubert, the adorable little brunette secretary with the dancing brown eyes, who worked in the home office. George Butler had promised that if I had a great summer, he would get me a date with her. Ah, yes, life was great.

Thump, thump, thump. At first I tried to ignore

the noise that was coming from under the back end of the car, but as the vibrations got rougher, I pulled onto the shoulder. I walked all around the Olds, kicking at the tires, but there was no flat. I started off again, but the thump, thump persisted. I decided I'd better not take any chances and pulled into a service station. The mechanic unhooked the trailer and put the car up on the rack.

"How far do you have to go?" he drawled.
"Nashville."
"That's all?"
"Yeah."
"No problem. You'll make it."
"You're sure?"
"Yeah."

So we hooked the trailer back up and off I went. About two or three miles down the road, I braked to slow down on a hill and realized I had no brakes! Fortunately I hadn't been going too fast. Then I pulled onto the shoulder of the road until the car slowed to a stop.

I sat there a minute, giving my heart time to slow back down, when a man came running up, yelling at the top of his voice: "Get out of there! Quick! There are flames shooting five feet out the back! Now, move!"

As I jumped out, I spotted the flames coming from under the car, blazing all around my gas tank. *This baby is fixing to explode!* I thought.

"Unhook your trailer! Get your stuff out of the car! Move!" the man ordered as he proceeded to unhook the trailer. "I'm an ex-police officer—I know what I'm doing. Now, hurry up!"

I started grabbing clothes and throwing them.

Principle 7: Let God Help You

Every time I put my head inside that car to grab more things, I thought the car would blow. The ex-officer assured me that cars explode only in the movies and on TV, but I didn't feel very secure about it. If he hadn't been so confident, I wouldn't have touched it. I managed to get most of my clothes out of the car while he disengaged the trailer. Within three minutes the car was totally engulfed in flames.

Then I remembered the $600 in checks in the glove compartment. I'd paid only $300 for the car, but the checks brought my loss up to about $900. I just stood there and watched it all burn. The traffic was stopped as far back as I could see. People got out of their cars and milled around, watching that baby burn. The horn was blowing in a dying protest at its untimely end.

It was an interesting contrast. A half hour before, I'd been on top of the world. Now I was watching my transportation turn to ashes amidst the commotion of all the people walking around. One lady came running up and stood right next to me. "It's burning! It's burning!" she wailed. "Who's car is that?"

"Mine."

"Yours! That car is yours! It's going to burn!"

"Ma'am, thank you very much, but it is already burning. If you will look closely, it has already burned." She was so overly concerned that I had to laugh a bit at her agitation.

"Oh, my! What are you going to do?"

"That's a very good question. I'm not sure. I'm just thankful I wasn't in the car. Thankful we got the trailer unhooked."

"How can you be so calm?"

"Well, Ma'am," I said grinning at her, "it's a long

story, but I've learned to accept my situation exactly as it is. . . ."

She looked at me as if I were crazy, but for me everything was falling into place. My principles worked here, too! It suddenly dawned on me that the seven principles that had helped me turn my life around weren't just for selling—or for managing. They were principles for living that could be applied to any situation or profession. That revelation meant more to me than the loss of the car or the inconvenience of having to hire someone to haul me and my trailer into Nashville. I'd learned seven principles of successful living!

I was filled with a great sense of gratitude, for it was surely the seventh principle—"Let God Help You"—that had made it possible for me to bounce back. Just a few months before, my confidence had been at an all-time low. I had had little hope of recovering financially and a lot of fear about the future. Yet God had helped me to accept my situation the way it was. Then he'd given me the courage to be willing to fail. He had helped me discipline myself to make daily preparations on a consistent basis. He'd given me the strength to work professionally to pace myself to do whatever needed to be done. Through his grace I had been able to live in the present and take it one day at a time throughout the summer. Most of all, God had enabled me to do my best.

Early into the summer while I was driving to Nashville, I had prayed "Lord, you know I believe in you, although I don't always show it. Thank you for being faithful even during my times of unfaithfulness. Forgive me for my inconsistencies.

Principle 7: Let God Help You

"I don't know how I'm going to get through this summer, but it says in Philippians 4:13 that I can do all things through Christ who strengthens me, and I choose to believe that. Please give me the strength to work hard, stay on schedule, and do my best, regardless of what I sell. I believe you will."

And he did. And he'll help you too, *if you'll let him.*

Does this mean that the six previous principles are invalid without faith in God? No, definitely not! But, I found that for me personally the chances of being able to apply the principles consistently are much greater with God's help.

Coach Bob Davenport has been one of the greatest influences in my life. All through college he was a living example of what God can do in a life. I'll never forget the day he said to me, "Dave, I know it looks to you as if the All-American honors and my pro ball experiences would be exciting. They're OK, but fleeting, and I can honestly tell you that there is nothing more exciting than a personal relationship with Jesus Christ."

He went on to explain that during his freshman year at UCLA he had taken a course sponsored by the newly organized Campus Crusade for Christ: "It was a rather unique, but not overly religious, group, and it afforded me the opportunity of seriously investigating the possibility of Christ being what he claimed to be—the Son of God. After completing UCLA, I realized that of all the courses I'd taken in earning my degree, that noncredit course taught by Dr. Bill Bright had been the most important, significant, and life-changing of all."

Over the years I've had this same truth reemphasized by many others. One of the most inspiring testimonies was that of Jim Irwin when he shared his experiences about his trip to the moon: "When I looked out and saw the earth only as big as a little marble, I thought, *How big am I? I'm just a speck of dust —if that big—compared to the universe.* And yet this little speck has the capacity to know God! To know the One who holds the universe. To know his love, and have his direction. For the first time I saw—*felt* —God's love for the earth, and John 3:16 took on a special significance: For God so loved the world that he gave his one and only Son that whoever believes in him shall not perish, but have eternal life. I realized then that God loved that little blue marble. That little planet. He loved all the billions of people on it. And he loved me!

"I realized that my relationship with Jesus Christ was the most precious thing I had, and I renewed that relationship on my journey to the moon."

It isn't necessary to take a trip to the moon to come to the same conclusion Jim did. Shortly after Don Thoren had been elected president of the National Speakers Association, he shared with me: "My life tends not to have traumatic turning points, but evolution. When I started out in business, I decided my theme song was going to be 'I Did It My Way.' I looked on Christians as a bunch of cripples who had to blame their failure or success on someone other than themselves.

"Then in a slow but steady way I found myself coming closer to the Lord. Picking up a Bible in a hotel room and reading from it occasionally, going to church once in a while, and talking with a fraternity brother from college, I finally came to realize that I could not earn a relationship with the Lord. I could

Principle 7: Let God Help You

only accept it. In a hotel room in Minneapolis, Minnesota, I told the Lord that I wanted to accept his gift of salvation, and was turning my life over to him.

"There was no ringing of bells, but there was a great transition in my life. I was no longer afraid. I quit worrying about myself and whether I would be a success. He gave me serenity."

While it is a great advantage to begin your relationship with God at an early age, it is not necessarily a prerequisite to success. Colonel Sanders had had a great deal of success before he "took God" as his partner. "At age seventy-nine, I had accomplished a great deal in business," he told me, "yet I still sensed a void. Something was not quite right. Then I attended a revival service in a church that was not even of my faith. Since the decision I made that night, I have had an assurance God's gonna take care of me."

Even though Dean Jones was making $15,000 a week, he told me, he was once so depressed that he stood at a motel window one night and thought, *If something doesn't happen in my life, I'm gonna blow the top of my head off.*

"What caused such dissatisfaction with life?" I asked him.

"I don't really know, Dave, but there was an emptiness I was constantly trying to fill. The more success and money I had, the more miserable I seemed to become. Anyone who wants to make it in show business feels that will satisfy him, but it doesn't. Money and fame can be nice, but they simply do not satisfy. I have since found that God is the only true source of fulfillment and satisfaction."

Dean Jones just contemplated suicide, but Marijohn Wilkin actually attempted it. "I don't know much about guns," she confided, "but one Easter morning I was so despondent I put a bullet in this gun, a long gun, not a handgun. I leaned over the barrel and pushed the trigger, and the bullet did the craziest thing. It deflected under my chin and landed on the floor. I tried it again and exactly the same thing happened. I looked up and said, 'Hey, God, I believe you are trying to tell me something.'

"Then I thought I had to figure why God had kept me from dying. My depression stopped, and I became more aware of everything around me. I started reading something besides *Billboard* and Mickey Spillane murder mysteries. I did hours and hours of study, going through various religions in search of something to fulfill my needs. Then songs like 'One Day at a Time' started pouring out, and I truly 'Returned to the God of My Childhood.' "

It isn't necessary to become desperate before turning to God for help. John Naber was still in high school when he heard a speaker who made him stop and consider the direction his life was going. "I was never a boozer or a drug addict," he recalls, "but I sensed a need in my life. One night in the privacy of my own bedroom, I prayed, *God, if you're real, let me know.* The immediate response after that was an assurance that he was there. It's my faith in his presence and sovereignty over my life that enables me to handle adversity as well as success. God promises some things. He loves me. I don't have to earn his love. He puts sports and everything else into proper perspective and allows us to get the most out of life."

"A young friend introduced me to the Bible when I was twenty-two," Charlie "Tremendous" Jones told me. "He left me alone. I read John 1:12, 3:16, and

Principle 7: Let God Help You

5:24, and then I accepted Christ. I was young and healthy, had a great future and a fine wife, but I knew from the Scriptures that I also had a great need. A motivator could have reached my head with that thought, but it took the Bible to reach my heart.

"I talk to businessmen all the time who think they don't need God. I just tell them, 'That's wonderful. Hang in there as long as you can, and do all you can to keep away from God. You don't need God to be happy and make money. I got all I needed without God.'

"But the fellow without God knows in his heart that he's a dead man. He knows he's got a happy act—nothing more. The time will come when he realizes he can't go on in his own strength, and then he'll find it easy and wonderful to receive Christ as Savior."

Cheryl Prewitt Blackwood tells of accepting Christ when she was fourteen. "I made this quiet decision to accept him—a quality decision. See, a lot of people grow up in church, and they know that Jesus loves them and that he died for all the world, but they've never realized that he's done it *for* them. If I were the only person on the earth, he would have done it for me.

"Jesus wasn't a pushy person. He never screamed and yelled and made people follow him. He led a quiet life, and if they followed him, they followed him. He never forced people to decide. But when we realize that we need him and want him to forgive the mess we've made of our lives, then he will. It's that simple."

"I'd heard about Jesus all my life, but I didn't really know who he was until I was thirty-four," Coach Tom Landry said. "I'd accomplished everything I'd set out to do in sports, yet there was a void in my life. I was going to quit football because I'd done everything in coaching I could do. I had a restlessness and emptiness before I discovered Christ.

"Then I began attending a Bible study group. I thought I knew all the Bible I needed. I knew the Easter story and the Christmas story, but I didn't even know the gospel of Jesus Christ—that he had died for me. When I discovered that, I made a commitment, and he filled the vacuum in my life.

"Now I realize that a person without Christ is handicapped. See, God made us in his image, and he made us unique. Therefore, we're going to find fulfillment in life only through a right relationship with God through Jesus Christ. Once we do that, we won't worry as much, and we'll have the capability of coming closer to reaching our God-given potential. Anyone who hasn't made that discovery is handicapped even if he doesn't realize it."

"I was always known as one who attended church," John Wooden told me. "However, it was mostly for appearances' sake, until I accepted Christ in my late thirties. I've found that the committed Christian can accept adversity and failure better than someone who is not committed to Christ."

As he was talking, he slowly pulled a little cross out of his pocket and placed it in my hand. "When I entered the service in 1943," Coach Wooden explained, "my minister gave me this little cross that he hoped would help me in times of tension. I've carried this cross with me ever since. It's a simple reminder of the fact that I'm a Christian. It isn't magic and it isn't meant to protect me from every physical harm; it's just a reminder. Whenever I'm under any sort of

Principle 7: Let God Help You

emotional pressure, it gives me a better realization of the Someone who is in control. It *reminds* me of the life-changing decision I made years ago."

Looking at the cross in my hand reminded me of another destiny-changing decision made upon a rocky hill outside Jerusalem long ago. Three men were being executed in a cold, heartless manner that day while the bloodthirsty mob jeered uncompassionately. A sign had been posted upon the center cross with a message written in three languages: THIS IS THE KING OF THE JEWS.

One of the victims, his face distorted as much by hate as by fear and pain, joined the mocking crowd in scoffing at the Man on the center cross. "So, you're the Messiah, are you? Prove it by saving yourself—and us, too, while you're at it!"

There was no reply from the battered form in the center of the scene, but strangely, the third man rose to his defense. "Don't you even fear God when you're dying?" he demanded of the mocker. "We deserve to die for our evil deeds, but this man hasn't done one thing wrong." Accepting his situation—hopeless though it seemed—he turned to the gentle-faced Man, who had been so cruelly disfigured. "Jesus, remember me when you come into your Kingdom."

With tender eyes, Jesus looked at the dying thief and promised, "Today you will be with me in Paradise."

The conversation lasted only thirty seconds, but a destiny was changed *forever.*

To the Reader

So, how can you get the most from this gold mine you hold in your hand?

Go back and review each chapter. You might want to devote a week or more to the first one, seeking the best method for you to work that particular principle into your own life. Then, go on to the second ... and the third. In two months or less, you might not recognize yourself and your accomplishments as your income and your desire to excel increase.

Og Mandino

For information regarding personal appearances, contact Dave Dean at the following address:

The Southwestern Company
P.O. Box 820
Nashville, TN 37211